My Heart
is
Bleeding

My Heart is Bleeding

is

The Life of
Dorothy
Squires

JOHNNY TUDOR

The
History
Press

Cover illustration: Film star Roger Moore plays the piano for his wife, singer Dorothy Squires. (John Pratt/Keystone Features/Getty Images)

First published 2017

The History Press
The Mill, Brimscombe Port
Stroud, Gloucestershire, GL5 2QG
www.thehistorypress.co.uk

British Library Cataloguing in Publication Data.
A catalogue record for this book is available from the British Library.

ISBN 978 0 7509 7900 9

Typesetting and origination by The History Press
Printed and bound by TJ International Ltd

Contents

Foreword

After the success of *Say It With Flowers*, the play I wrote about Dorothy Squires with my good friend Meic Povey, many people have expressed a wish to know more about this talented, controversial and sometimes difficult Welsh woman. Having the advantage of knowing Dorothy for most of my life and the benefit of access to her personal letters and reminiscences given to me by her niece, Emily Squires, has given me a first-hand and sometimes emotional insight into her story that allowed me to open up untold layers of this dramatic life. I was also privileged to have recorded interviews with Dorothy just before she died. Consequently, her quotes give this book an authenticity, which I would not have been able to achieve had it not been for the 5 hours of recorded dialogue in my possession.

My life has been inextricably linked with Dorothy's and although I feature quite heavily in this book, it's not my story; it's Dorothy's story seen through my eyes. At times it reads like a Greek tragedy – her relentless journey from rags to riches and back again seems at times to be like a ridiculous parody – but there are great moments of joy and humour too. So, as you turn the pages of this book, I hope my efforts bring to life the excitement of the good times when Dorothy was riding high, as well as the trials and tribulations of her journey from humble beginnings in the South Wales Valleys to the pinnacle of international stardom. It was a privilege to be with Dorothy at the end and, although the manner of her passing was sad, I will always remember her as the vibrant woman she once was, how I learnt from her and how she touched all our lives back then.

Acknowledgements

This book would never have been written without the encouragement and friendship of the television producer Peter Edwards, who had the vision and confidence in my ability to write it and my friend Emily Squires, who gave me access to Dot's personal letters and reminiscences and trusted me to portray her aunt's life accurately and honestly. I am most grateful to them and the people who gave up their time to relay their memories of Dorothy to me. In particular Dorothy's friend and musical director Ernie Dunstal; John Lloyd, her publicist and loyal fan, who is sadly no longer with us; Hilda Brown her secretary and Peter Bennett a stalwart friend and confidant, who with his partner Des Brown were there for her when she needed it most.

1

The First Meeting

LONDON 1961

See Him Rog? I knew him when I had big tits and straw in my hair.

These were the first words I ever heard Dorothy Squires utter. She was walking down Wardour Street in the West End with her then husband Roger Moore and her recording manager Norman Newell, when she spotted my father and me. 'My lovely Bert,' she squealed. Then, totally ignoring Roger, gave my father a smacker of a wet kiss. I was an 18-year-old stage-struck kid in London for an audition that day so you can imagine how blown away I was, not only by Dorothy's mesmerising personality but by meeting The Saint himself. This was pre-Bond but Roger was already a big star.

Dorothy and Roger were on their way to a private showing of a film called *Tammy Tell Me True*, starring Sandra Dee and John Gavin. Dorothy had written the theme tune for it and she was on a terrific high. So, still ignoring Roger, she invited … no, demanded that we go with her to the champagne reception. After too much champagne and the 2-hour film, we emerged blinkingly and half-cut into the harsh daylight of the street. A bunch of young girls immediately surrounded Roger pleading for his autograph. We walked on with Dorothy who pretended not to notice the gaggle of giggling girls then, turning to Roger, she yelled 'come on you prick we'll be late.' I was to realise later that her total indifference to Roger's star status was because their marriage was on the rocks. Roger, ever the gentleman, graciously extricated himself from his adoring fans and joined us but it was obvious things weren't right – not long after that their much publicised break-up hit the press. Putting on a brave face, Dorothy linked arms with my father and me and announced in a commanding voice that we were all going to Raymond's Revue Bar – she'd booked a table to celebrate. So, with Dorothy taking the lead, we made our way to Soho. I'd never seen a place like it. Its intoxicating atmosphere engulfed me.

Soho pulsed with life in those days. Flashing neon signs advertised adult entertainment: strip clubs, massage parlours, adult bookshops and the like. Touts were standing in doorways of sleazy clubs. 'Come inside, they are naked and they move,' they bawled to anyone within earshot. Situated adjacent to these clubs was one of the more respectable if not entirely innocent venues in Soho, the Windmill Theatre, where comedians battled valiantly to get laughs from jaded mainly male audiences in grubby raincoats. The only time the comics would raise a titter – if you'll excuse the expression – was when the men, having sat through all five shows to ogle the girls, would see one of the artists going wrong. An alternative source of entertainment was when someone would vacate a front row seat and a stampede would ensue to claim it; men would clamber over the backs of seats to get a better view of the naked girls standing motionless in tableaus. Outside the stage door chorus boys lounged, still with their make-up on, having a well-earned fag – the tobacco variety of course.

Opposite, in Archer Street, stood a group of musicians on the short stretch of pavement between Great Windmill Street and Rupert Street. I asked Dorothy what they were doing. She told me that they were collecting their pay. 'As long as I can remember,' she said, 'musicians have gathered on Mondays to collect their fee from previous gigs and see if there was any work for the coming week. It was like a club; they meet to share stories about gigs, club owners, and just generally shoot the breeze.' Dorothy knew all this stuff because she'd started out as a band singer when she was a kid; in her words she was one of the boys and often preferred to travel on the band bus with the musicians than travel in her own car.

Across the road from Archer Street was our destination; a huge red neon sign flashed announcing Raymond's Revue Bar. The club was the creation of property magnate and magazine publisher Paul Raymond for whom some years later I worked in another of his venues – the Celebrity Restaurant. It was at the Celebrity that Dorothy met and fell for another of her beaus Keith Miller but more of that later. The Revue Bar offered traditional burlesque-style entertainment, which included strip tease. It was popular with leading entertainment figures of the day and was one of the few legal venues in London to show full-frontal nudity by turning itself into a members-only club. I asked Dot if she was a member. She said she didn't need to be; her face was her membership. So, ignoring the doorman she made a grand entrance with the rest of us trailing in her wake.

We were shown to our table. More champagne was ordered and Dorothy proceeded to regale us of how writing the theme for the film we'd just seen had all come about. While she was in Hollywood, she'd heard that Ross Hunter, the Oscar-nominated director of *Airport* and *Pillow Talk* had been looking for a theme for his picture so she set about writing it. When she'd finished she sent Roger over to Universal International with the manuscript and hoped for the best. There were two songs shortlisted and Dorothy's was one of them. At five o'clock that day she received a call from the studio to say her theme had been chosen; it was in the picture. Dorothy was ecstatic and recalled:

And you imagine what I was like? There were seven workmen in the house, I got them all drunk. I used the Vintage champagne, Roger nearly killed me. They [the workmen] didn't know what it was all about. The next day there I was, eight o'clock in the morning on the sound stage of Universal International in a headscarf and slacks listening to a sixty-piece orchestra conducted by Percy Faith. They were playing my tune. It was one of the biggest thrills of my life and the icing on the cake was the $2,000 in advance of royalties I was paid.

Dorothy, like most Celts, was a good storyteller so, as we quaffed more of her champagne, she proceeded to entertain us with more tales of Hollywood. Roger had of course heard it all before but this didn't deter her; she was the centre of attention now and loving it. In England she was Dorothy Squires not, in her words, 'Mrs Roger Bloody Moore'. I was too young to realise what she meant by that remark but in retrospect I think she resented the fact that her star status had been eclipsed by her handsome and much younger husband.

I only met Roger that one time and I was a little overawed by being in the presence of a superstar. Remember, I was this young gauche kid with theatrical aspirations carrying a portfolio of publicity photos but Roger had a great way of making one feel at ease in his presence. Dorothy insisted he take a look at my pictures and he picked one out of me doing an impression of Sammy Davis Jnr. Later, when he was thumbing through a magazine he found a picture of Sammy and quipped, 'Hey John, there's a bloke here taking the piss out of you.'

That first encounter was the beginning of a lifelong and sometimes difficult friendship with Dorothy. It's funny how some people's lives get intrinsically linked with someone else; I seemed to have been linked with Dorothy all my adult life, from that first meeting in London until her sad demise in April 1998 at Llwynypia Hospital.

Dorothy was a paradoxical character – a mixture of Auntie Mame and Cruella de Vil – when she was on form there was no better company; I have fond memories of her entertaining us with her colourful stories of Hollywood and all the film stars she knew. But Dot had a dark side; she could fly off the handle at the least provocation and reduce you to tears with one of her vitriolic jibes. On the other hand she was generous and kind; her impressive mansion in Bexley was an open house to any lame duck that needed a bed for the night. She wasn't a very good judge of character though and was often taken for granted by all the sycophantic hangers-on hoping to be the next Roger Moore.

While I was appearing at the Pigalle, a nightclub in London's West End, Dot insisted I stay with her at St Mary's Mount, her grand house in Bexley, and The Mount became my home whenever I was in London. I couldn't believe my luck; I was only on fifty quid a week and I was living in a twenty-two-roomed mansion with a swimming pool. One night during the performance at the Pigalle a message came backstage that Dorothy was out front with the producer of the show, Robert Nesbit. She wanted me to join them. It's an unwritten rule of the theatre that you never go out front during a performance but Dorothy assured me that she'd cleared it with the management and so out I went. It turned out to be a very embarrassing experience; Dot had had a drink or two that night and was being a bit discourteous towards Mr Nesbitt: 'Do you remember when you fucked up the lighting for a show in Las Vegas, Robert? No wonder they call you the Prince of fucking Darkness!'

I didn't know where to put myself, this was my boss she was insulting and a very important man in show business; he was the producer of the Royal Command Performance for goodness sake! I needn't have worried though; Robert just laughed and said 'you're incorrigible Dorothy'. Robert Nesbit was a gent. After a six-month run at the Pigalle I went into a musical called *Cindy* at the Fortune Theatre in Covent Garden. The assistant stage manager was a young fella called Cameron Mackintosh – I wonder what happened to him! Dorothy insisted on coming to the opening night but I didn't really want her to come; I knew how outspoken she was and I was worried in case she would upset someone. She sat in the circle with my father and when I did my big number she started yelling encore at the top of her voice and whistling. This was the second time she'd embarrassed me but this time it had a positive effect; the audience picked up on it and I got a standing ovation. Inadvertently she'd done me a favour and we drove back to St Mary's Mount to celebrate.

St Mary's Mount – Bexley

I have some great memories of that large Victorian pile set in 4 acres with its lawns sweeping down to the swimming pool and orchards beyond. I lived in a council flat with my parents in Port Talbot at the time so this palatial mansion with its *Gone With The Wind* staircase, nine bedrooms, oak-lined dining room, snooker room, bar as big as any pub, library and huge ranch-style lounge was a magical place to me. Dorothy had added the Ranch-style room to this already enormous house without planning permission. Dorothy never asked permission to do anything. When she had to fill her swimming pool she just put a hosepipe in it and let it run for weeks. She should have called the fire brigade and paid them to fill it, after all it took 33,000 gallons but she continued to do this until the Water Board, who thought there was a leak, turned up and threatened to take action.

The house was always full of people. There were never less than ten for Sunday lunch. Dorothy would also throw parties for the world and his wife, where one would rub shoulders with the great and the good of show business: Shirley Bassey, Diana Dors, Tony Hatch, Jackie Trent, Peggy Mount, Lionel Bart et al. I remember being taken aback by how posh William Bramble was and not a bit like his character in the situation comedy *Steptoe and Son*, save for how his ill-fitting false teeth would drop when he spoke, reminiscent of Old Man Steptoe himself.

Another real character that stayed with Dorothy was Rex Jameson, who was often on Dorothy's variety bills. His alter ego was Mrs Shufflewick or Shuff, as he was affectionately known. The character he portrayed on stage was an old cockney woman in the snug of her local pub called The Cock & Comfort: 'A lot of comfort, but not much of anything else,' he would quip. Shuff had a bit of a drink problem. When Dot paid him on a Friday he would post himself some money to the next theatre so he wouldn't spend it all on booze. When he would turn up at Bexley he'd go straight to the bar and drink a bottle of sherry straight down and Dorothy would have to put him on the train for home blind drunk. Shuff was always grateful for Dot's kindness and would invariably leave a present as a thank you for her hospitality. Little did she know at the time that Shuff had nicked it from the Army and Navy Stores.

Dorothy's parties were wild affairs; if not exactly *Valley of the Dolls*, they weren't mother's union soirées either. You never knew where you would be sleeping or with whom. When all the beds were full, people could be seen fornicating al fresco in the flora and fauna.

When things got a little too wild, which was often, I would make my excuses to Dot and sojourn to the office. I slept in the office most times. One night I was aware of a vertically challenged refugee from *Snow White* who was a little worse for wear. He staggered into the office mumbling that he couldn't find the toilet. I pointed him towards the door but he opened the wrong one and fell down the cellar. I expect the next pantomime performance was *Snow White and the Six Dwarfs*. Everyone who went to Dot's parties had to do a turn and Emily Squires, Dorothy's niece, remembers:

> Dorothy had set up a microphone in the white room and the guests were taking it in turns to sing. Dorothy sang first followed by Shirley Bassey then Diana Dors. I was only a teenager but I remember feeling sorry for Diana, having to follow two of the most powerful singers in show business; she should have gone on first. During the impromptu karaoke session Lionel Bart sat with Shirley Bassey's first husband, Kenneth Hume, and I remember thinking that it was strange him wearing make-up and in the day time too.

Dorothy asked Jacky Trent to get up to sing but she declined saying she had a bad throat. Dorothy, not one to mince her words, told her she'd never be a singer as long as she had a hole up her arse then turning to me said 'give us a song John,' and had the cheek to ask Jacky's husband Tony Hatch, the record producer and songwriter, to accompany me on the piano.

At another party I was sat next to a skinny, morose looking man with a black curly perm wearing sunglasses. I asked Dot who the strange looking guy was. She told me it was Phil Spector the famous, or by now the infamous, murderous music mogul and record producer of the *Wall of Sound* fame – Dot knew everybody. Well … I say she knew everybody; one guy called Eddie would turn up with his case and move in for a few days, do a bit of work around the house and then leave. Nobody seemed to know who the hell he was; he was just Eddie. Another uninvited guest to St Mary's Mount was a ghost – Dot swore the house was haunted; she even got a priest in to exorcise the place. Lights would go on and off for no apparent reason and Dot's sister, Rene, swore she felt little feet running over her when she was in bed. Dorothy swore it was Sir Arthur Conan Doyle who was rumoured to have lived there – but I think it was Eddie!

I saw so many famous people pass through Dot's house: Tony Hancock, the biggest TV and radio star of the fifties and sixties, escaped from a drying out clinic in Brighton and turned up at St Mary's Mount seeking sanctuary; he was accompanied by the wife of John Le Mesurier (Sergeant Wilson of *Dad's Army* fame) with whom it transpired, he'd been having an affair.

Tony was in a terrible state; he had the DTs and his body was covered with scabs. Dorothy, taking pity on him, told him he could stay until he could sort himself out and made up a bed in the library – big mistake – he drank a bottle of scotch and half a bottle of gin that had been inadvertently left there. The next morning Dot was awoken by the apparition of a naked Tony Hancock, hovering next to her bed, his ample appendage dangling far too close for comfort in front of her eyes. The unshockable Dorothy, flicking the mammoth member away said 'get that out of my face' and accepted the tea he was offering with grace. Then, seeing the humour in the situation, quipped 'Who's your tailor?' The next day Dorothy took a phone call from John Le Mesurier. Tearfully he explained that he'd heard through the grapevine that his wife was at St Mary's Mount with Hancock and what should he do about it. 'Why are you asking me?' she said, 'I've really fucked up my life good and proper.' Then as an afterthought, told him to put a new song in his act, and put the phone down.

Later, Dorothy received a phone call from Billy Marsh, Tony's agent. He'd also heard that Tony was at Dorothy's and pleaded with her to keep him sober as he had an egg advert to do. She promised to do her best. She hid all the booze in her bar and plied him with coffee. When Tony's car came for him it was a beautiful navy blue drophead Rolls-Royce. Dorothy told Tony's driver that 'Mr Hancock has got an egg commercial to do, which will earn him a lot of money. So don't stop on the way to give him a drink.' But Dorothy hadn't accounted for the deviousness of a confirmed alcoholic. Tony bribed his chauffeur to smuggle in a half bottle of brandy and he drank it all before leaving for the studio. Dorothy called Billy and said 'you've had it, Billy, you'll have no commercial today'. Billy must have succeeded though, because Tony was to be seen 'going to work on an egg' and demanding 'Where are my soldiers?' on national television for the rest of the year.

Another time I stayed with Dorothy was when I was appearing at the Beaverwood Club, a stone's throw away from Bexley. I asked Dot if she would like to come one night and she told me that she was banned. It transpired that on Christmas Eve in 1965 Dorothy and Emily had gone to the club. Dot was accompanied by Tom Jones and Emily was accompanied by Viv Richards, a long-haired member of a pop group called the Pretty Things. Emily remembers Dorothy and Tom getting a bit too amorous – I wonder if he's put that in his book. They were being particularly loud and disruptive that night, which brought stares from the surrounding patrons and they were respectfully asked to leave.

Emily Squires was a regular visitor to Bexley. When her father (Dot's brother Fred) died, Emily's mother, Joyce Golding, a variety artist, was on tour with Max Miller so Emily was put into a convent at the tender age of 5. She told me the day her mother handed her over to the Reverend Mother she felt abandoned, alone and afraid. She very rarely saw Joyce and, except for the odd comic book she would receive through the post, there was very little contact. Dorothy became a sort of surrogate mother to her; in fact most people thought Dorothy *was* her mother.

She loved Emily like the daughter she never had, even offering to adopt her and every chance she got she would take her out of the convent and bring her back to Bexley. Emily, like me, thought St Mary's Mount was a magical place and a wonderful place to grow up. As a child she would dress up in all of Dorothy's pantomime clothes that were kept in huge wardrobe skips under the stairs, play in the woods with her friend Carl and swim in the pool. She recalled with love the way she would sit in the empty pool as it was being filled and rise to the top with the water.

One memorable event Emily recalls is when Dorothy and Roger turned up at Our Ladies' Convent to watch her singing in a school concert. They arrived in their powder blue Ford Thunderbird convertible; Dorothy dressed in a mink coat and diamante glasses and Roger in his Saville Row suit. They stuck out like sore thumbs amongst the other parents. Dorothy proceeded to make a spectacle of herself as usual. She was like Rosalind Russell in *Gypsy* giving instructions to Emily from the audience but instead of yelling out 'sing out Louise', she was yelling, 'Sing out Emily Jane', much to Emily's embarrassment. To make amends she invited four nuns and six kids to Bexley for the day. It was a lovely day; the pool had just been filled and Roger was dispatched to get ice cream for everyone. The kids, not having swimming costumes with them, raided Dorothy's knicker drawer and jumped squealing with delight into the water clad in an assortment of Dorothy's multicoloured knickers.

Emily told me that her relationship with Dorothy was idyllic whilst she was a child but as soon as she reached puberty Dorothy treated her more like a companion than a teenager. She took her to places that in many people's eyes were not suitable for a girl of such tender years who'd been brought up in a convent. Dorothy even took the unsuspecting Emily to see an X-rated movie at the Windmill because an actor Dot had been out with was in it and she'd heard there was a great shot of his bum.

Emily, having been exposed to the world of showbiz from a young age, had grown up fast. When she was only 8, she'd inadvertently whistled in the dressing room, a heinous crime amongst the theatrical fraternity. Like most people in showbiz, Dorothy always adhered to the superstitions of the theatre and ordered Emily to go outside, turn round three times, swear then come back in. When Emily protested that she didn't know any swear words, Dot told her to try bollocks.

Emily often went with Dorothy to Denmark Street, the little street off Tottenham Court Road affectionately known as Tin Pan Alley. It was the hub of the music business in those days, frequented by recording managers, songwriters, pop groups and song pluggers. There was a real buzz about the place with its music shops and small recording studios, where hopefuls could make an acetate disc of their latest song and try to sell it to one of the publishers. Wannabes would hang out in a coffee bar called La Giaconda hoping to be discovered. Everybody congregated in that little coffee bar or The White Lion pub at the other end of the street and it was here that Emily met and fell for a young rock drummer. This became a bone of contention between Dot and Em; Dorothy didn't like the fact that he was married, which was rich coming from her; she'd lived with a married man for twelve years before meeting Roger, with whom she started having an affair whilst *he* was still married to his first wife.

Emily could give as good as she got though, and was probably the only one who would tell Dorothy the truth and not what she wanted to hear. This often led to heated screaming matches, which sometimes became violent, leading to Emily walking out. One particularly pernicious punch-up occurred in The White Lion. Emily was having dinner with Dorothy when, after a few glasses of wine, Dorothy started insulting Emily's boyfriend by calling him 'An ignorant cockney cunt'. Emily retaliated, telling her not to call her boyfriend a cunt. Dorothy, mishearing the comment, thought Emily had called *her* a cunt and war broke out. She took a swing at Emily and caught her hairpiece, which went flying and landed in some bloke's Boef Bourguignon. Emily made a dash for the ladies' followed hot foot by Dorothy. With flailing fists, she set about her cowering niece; her diamond encrusted ring cutting Emily's face. Emily, being twice the size of her diminutive aunt pinned her against the wall and started shouting for help. Two music publishers, hearing the rumpus, rushed into the ladies', grabbed Dot before she could do any more damage and Emily escaped, with Dot yelling, 'Fuck off, I've been looking at my brother's face for too long,' ringing in her ears. Make of that outburst what you will. To me, it was as if Emily reminded Dorothy of her brother Fred, who also wouldn't take any shit from her. Fred was 6ft 2in but this didn't deter Dorothy from standing on a chair to hit him on the head with her stiletto-heeled shoe yelling, 'Take that, Captain cunt'.

Dorothy didn't see Emily for months after the incident in The White Lion. She tried calling her every day, leaving messages but Emily wasn't returning her calls. Dorothy was always sorry after her outbursts and would try anything to make amends. So, in desperation she wrote her a letter, which read:

The wall flowers miss you, the dog misses you, the cat misses you, the washing machine misses you; in fact, we all fucking miss you.

After every bust-up, which were legion, Emily would inevitably be drawn back to St Mary's Mount by Dorothy's Svengali-like magnetism and everything would seemingly go back to normal – if you can call living with Dorothy normal. And so, Emily resumed her role as companion, accompanying Dorothy on her trips to her favourite haunts, one of them being the A&R Club, which was situated on top of Francis, Day and Hunter, the music publishers in Tottenham Court Road. It had a colourful clientele, being the preferred watering hole for some of London's prime villains, madams, musicians and singers from Tin Pan Alley and actors like Kenneth Williams and Ronnie Frazer. The club was owned by stage and TV star Barbara Windsor's first husband, the infamous Ronnie Knight, who was rumoured to have been linked to the gangland slaying of Italian Tony. Ronnie admitted in his recent autobiography, *Memoirs and Confessions*, that he had ordered Mr Tony Zomparelli's killing in 1970. He said the Italian-born gangster was assassinated in revenge for the murder of his brother, David, who died after a fight at the Latin Quarter nightclub in London's West End.

One particular night, when Dot and Emily were having a drink in the A&R Club, a man ran through the bar being pursued by a knife-wielding gangster. He jumped through the window landed on the sun canopy below then jumped to the ground and beat a hasty retreat. What was amazing is that no one took a blind bit of notice; they just carried on drinking as if it were a normal occurrence. Mickey Regan, Ronnie Knight's business partner, turned to Emily, patting what can only be described as a gun-shaped bump beneath his jacket, and said 'Don't worry Em if anyone touches you, you just tell your uncle Mickey'. Dorothy, having over imbibed of the Amontillado Sherry, decided it was time to go. Exiting the club she saw a taxi that wasn't displaying a light. Undeterred by the fact that the taxi wasn't for hire, she got in. The driver, who just happened to be the actor, Bernard Breslaw's brother, Stanley, told her he was off duty. Dorothy, who was in a particularly cantankerous mood that night, refused point blank to get out and gave instructions to be taken to the Embassy Club. No amount of cajoling could persuade her to leave, so Stanley attempted to bodily drag her out.

She fought like a wildcat resulting in Stanley being kicked in the head. Bleeding, he returned to his seat, locked the doors and drove the disruptive diva to Strand Police Station where she was charged with 'Unlawful assault, hereby causing actual bodily harm, contrary to Section 47 of the offences against the persons act'. She was fined costs of £130.

Dorothy seemed to like being linked with dangerous characters, as a lot of showbiz personalities do. It was even rumoured that Dorothy had had an amorous assignation with one infamous gangster in her office in Oxford Street. (I won't mention which one it was as he may still be with us and I'm quite fond of my kneecaps.) Dorothy's predilection for gangsters intrigued me and I persuaded her to take me to a pub in the East End of London, which was believed to be frequented by the Kray Twins. I'd heard tales of London's gangland from my father, who'd been around in the days of Jack Spot, the king of London's gangland, before the Krays were born. Now I was about to experience it first-hand.

I was shivering with excitement as I followed Dorothy into the smokey up-beat atmosphere. The pub was full to bursting. The men had a charismatic if dangerous air about them with their large muscles and goodness knows what else bulging beneath their shiny mohair Italian-cut suits. The smell of sweat mingling with the scent of Old Spice and Californian Poppy, worn by the pretty mini-skirted girls with their beehive hairdos and winkle picker stiletto high-heeled shoes, only added to the sleazy but exciting atmosphere. Dorothy had heard that a jazz organist called Lennie Peters, whose uncle was Charlie Watts, the drummer of the Rolling Stones, was playing there that night and she wanted to check him out. Lennie had been blinded in a brawl when he was 16 but this didn't deter him from being a great keyboard player or, later, from becoming a huge star as part of a duo called Peters and Lee. As we listened to the sound of jazz coming from Lenny's Hammond organ, with its twin Leslie speakers spewing out the sound of 'The Cat' by Jimmy Smith, I could see why Dorothy found it exciting to be rubbing shoulders with the underworld; it was intoxicating. The colourful scene was reminiscent of a Damon Runyon novel. I was still high on the atmosphere when we returned to St Mary's Mount to drink tea in the tranquillity of Dot's kitchen.

2

The Early Years

The luxurious life at St Mary's Mount was a long way from the coal, tin and chapel culture of Llanelli: the Tin Works with its tall chimneys spewing out vast grey clouds that billowed and hung over the town, the row of terraced houses that clung to a mountainside, where Dorothy had been brought up, and the turbaned girl dressed in crossover overalls, who'd worked like an automaton on an assembly line. It had certainly been a long hard road from the Tin Plate Works to Tin Pan Alley. Life hadn't been easy for the young Edna May or Dorothy as she later became. Her story began with her birth in a gypsy caravan in Dafen, South Wales. She came from a showman family; her grandfather ran rides on Stutz Travelling Fairground and Archie, Edna's father, ran a coconut shy. Archie was a gambler and womaniser who was often absent, which made life tough for Dorothy's mother, who had to bring up Dorothy and her two siblings, Rene and Fred, virtually single-handed.

Dorothy was the rebel of the family. She wasn't content to fit in like the rest; she had theatrical ambitions. She'd got the bug for singing at an early age. She remembers the St David's Day school concert and schoolgirls wearing an assortment of daffodils and leeks, standing on a makeshift stage of railway sleepers. The diminutive Dorothy, dressed in a smock dress, jostled for position amongst the much bigger girls. She stumbled and fell, her little glasses trampled underfoot. She turned defiantly to face the much older girl, fists raised ready to fight for her position, her feisty spirit that would take her to the top of her profession evident even at that early age. Accompanied by an out of tune piano, the choir launched lustily into 'Calon Lân' but the only voice the audience were aware of was that of Dorothy's, pure and strong. She recalled:

> I was the only small kid in the choir – a little Dwt – the short arse with all the grown-ups. I had beautiful clothes. Dada loved me in my beautiful clothes but he'd never let me have shoes – always boots. I was like a fairy with little white boots. I remember the stage was made of railway sleepers that sounded like a xylophone when I walked on it.

At 15 Dorothy went to work in the tin plate factory but she was a free spirit and hated the confinement and discipline of the factory floor. Her only escape from the drudgery of the assembly line was the local fleapit of a cinema where she would watch spellbound as Al Jolson lit up the silver screen. She saw the Jolson Story twelve times. Seduced by the glitz of Hollywood she dreamed of becoming a star. She was often ridiculed by her workmates for her ambitions, which often led to full on fist fights and she bore the scars to prove it.

A cacophonous catfight started when a tough looking girl, fed up with Dot going on about being a singing star, told her that she'd never be a star as long as she had a hole up her arse. Dot made a grab for the girl and a lot of kicking and screaming broke out. The foreman tried to break it up and got a smack in the eye for his trouble. He told Dot that if she didn't toe the line he would have no alternative but to sack her. The uncompromising Dorothy told him to stick his fucking job, she didn't need it; she was going to be a star and she stormed out clutching yet another pair of smashed spectacles. This didn't go down too well at home, not only because of the loss of a much-needed wage but because the foreman just happened to be Dorothy's older sister Rene's husband, George.

Dorothy was now out of work but glad to be free of the factory. She kept body and soul together by babysitting, running errands and scrubbing kitchens. She would even forage for coal on the smouldering slag heaps that surrounded the town, resulting in her knees being peppered with indelible blue scars where the coal dust had penetrated her young skin. To say that Dorothy wasn't very good with money would be an understatement; as soon as she earned a few bob from her efforts she would blow it on the cinema. This extravagance would prove to be the pattern for her entire life and was undoubtedly a contributing factor in her eventual downfall.

Determined to break into show business she bought a battered old ukulele from a junk shop; she wanted a piano more than anything but her mother couldn't afford it so she had to do with a ukulele instead. She practiced singing Al Jolson songs in the Ty Bach – the toilet at the bottom of the garden – and would try out her new-found talent on the local boys of the village. Little did the naive Edna May realise they were more impressed by the size of her breasts than her vocal skills. When Dorothy joined a local dance band called the Denza Players, her father Archie was dead set against it. Being the womaniser that he was, he was frightened she would see him out at the local dance hall with his bit on the side. Dorothy undaunted, and aided and abetted by her long-suffering mother, would climb out of her bedroom window under cover of darkness. Her mother would lower her suitcase out of the window on a piece of rope and Dorothy would change in an adjacent phone box. It can't have been a nice experience stripping down to her underwear in a cold smelly phone box that had been used for activities other than communicating. Undaunted by the smell of bodily excretions, she would don her brown dance frock with a silver star on the front then totter off down the road in her dangerously high-heeled silver shoes to do her five-bob gig.

The rows with her father and the constant taunts of her friends took their toll and the situation for Edna May became intolerable. So, with little more than hope, courage and the price of a one-way ticket in her pocket she decided to leave for the bright lights of London. Dorothy left Llanelli early one morning before her father was up. An icy wind was blowing through the station, which was deserted save for a porter and a drunk sleeping it off on a bench. The 16-year-old Edna May, clutching her bag that contained her few meagre possessions, shivered more from excitement than cold as she contemplated the adventures that lay before her. Betty, her school friend from Pwll arrived just in time to see her off. They hugged each other for a moment and Dorothy, with tears in her eyes, promised that when she was a big star she'd send for her. As the steam-belching train bound for London pulled out of the station, Dorothy looked back to the already diminishing figure of Betty and wondered, for all her well-intentioned promises, if she would ever see her best friend again.

The cacophony of sound that assaulted her young ears on arriving at Paddington must have been intimidating – she'd never been further than Swansea before. Alone and friendless, she plunged into the big city dragging her one case with her. Finding B&B for 7/6, she dumped her case and clutching a letter of introduction from her old choirmaster she went in search of the Royal Academy of Music. Finding the imposing building, she nervously entered and asked for an audition. Standing in front of a panel of hardnosed academics must have been an intimidating experience for this naive little Welsh girl. I can only imagine what they must have thought when she opened a violin case, pulled out her battered ukulele and burst unceremoniously into 'Dinah is There Anyone Finer'. After she'd finished her rendition she was told by a sympathetic member of the panel that they thought she was in the wrong place. Dorothy apologised, saying she was sorry that she had bothered them. They said she hadn't bothered them but she'd certainly entertained them and suggested kindly that she try Charing Cross Road where all the theatrical agents were.

Frightened but determined, she tramped the streets looking for work. Her meagre savings were running out fast so she got a job as an auxiliary nurse at the Mayday Hospital, but she soon found out that slopping out bedpans and changing soiled patients wasn't for her so she hit the streets once more. Arriving at Charing Cross Road she discovered an old mansion block with a brass plaque that announced, amongst other things, Joe Kay, Theatrical Agent. It was a typical theatrical agent's office; the walls were decorated with playbills and pictures of the agent Joe Kay posing with celebrities of the day.

Above a large leather-topped desk was a photo of Joe sat behind a full set of drums, caught mid solo, his right stick crashing down onto the snare and the other spinning in his fingers high above his head. Joe was in deep discussion with Jack Lewis, who ran an act called Jack Lewis's Rolling Stones, when Dot burst unannounced into his office. Yes, there was a group called the Rolling Stones, before Mr Jagger took on the mantle. Dorothy spluttered in a strong Welsh accent 'Do you give audition yer?' She was about to get the bum's rush when my father, Bert Cecil, the pianist with the band, pleaded her case. She nervously handed Bert a tattered piece of music and burst lustily into 'Dinah is There Anyone Finer'. Joe was impressed by her voice but not with her choice of song; he didn't understand why she was singing a man's song. She explained it was because it was the first one that came into her head. Bert suggested that Joe book her a gig at the Osterley Hotel in the West End. Joe told my old man he was mashugana, 'No way am I going to put this girl with big tits and straw in her hair in one of my best dates.' I don't know whether it was because Bert recognised her Welsh accent or because he fancied her, but he offered to play for her if Joe gave her the date and if she didn't do any good he would do his act for nothing. Joe grudgingly relented and booked her for the Osterley for the princely sum of 30s. Dorothy never forgot Bert's kindness and he became her lifelong friend without whom, in her own words, she would have not made it in show business. Dorothy recalled that memorable day:

I couldn't believe it … Thirty bob! – I thought that was a fortune. So, I went out [of the office] and I told your father. And he said 'Where are you staying Dinah?' He always called me Dinah … because I sang the song see. Anyway, I told him my bags were in digs in Victoria but I couldn't afford to pay the landlady. Bert was always a soft touch for anyone down on their luck, so he came with me to the digs, paid the 7/6 I owed then said, 'Come on Dinah, let's go home to Mammy and Pop'. So he took me to his mother and father in Streatham. The whole band stayed with your grandmother … She was lovely. I stayed there for four months but I was getting in a rut; I had to go and earn some money. I owed her see, your Grandmother. I promised to pay her twenty-five bob a week when I got on my feet. We all called her Mammy; she was a wonderful lady.

My grandparents' house in Chaucer Road, Streatham, was always full of out of work band boys, including members of Jack Lewis's Rolling Stones. All the rooms were taken when Dorothy arrived so she had to sleep in the same room as my grandfather and grandmother. They were like a second mother and father to her and she affectionately called them Mammy and Pop for the rest of her life. Pop told me that she would often ask him to tell her Welsh stories, which reminded her of home and when she was in a mischievous mood she would say, 'Tell me some dirty yarns Pop'.

For all Bert's promises he couldn't be with her that night at the Osterley Hotel, he had another engagement and Dorothy had to face the ordeal of her first London gig alone. She arrived wearing a moth-eaten rabbit skin coat she'd picked up in a second-hand shop and a black dress she'd borrowed from Bert's sister. The Osterley was a plush West End hotel and Dorothy was very intimidated by its opulence. Stomach churning, she nervously hung back, watching as the well-heeled clientele handed in their very expensive coats to the hat check girl. When they had all cleared, Dorothy sheepishly handed in her moth-eaten coat and told the girl that she was singing there that night and asked where the dressing room was. The girl nodded towards a well-worn door – it turned out to be the kitchen. It was bedlam in there; waiters were throwing down trays and shouting orders, chefs were shouting back and slinging saucepans about and Dorothy half dressed, standing amongst the mayhem, was trying to explain her music to a not very interested pianist. He took the music and without looking at it walked away and exited through the swing doors, leaving Dorothy nervously contemplating how the sophisticated London audience would receive this little girl from Wales:

I'll never forget that night. The compère was quite nice but the pianist! Now … just remember, I'd never performed anywhere on my own before and the room was packed with holidaymakers. I was terrified; I went on the stage, the pianist played the introduction but I was paralysed with nerves; I couldn't remember the first line. I just stood there in a state of complete panic. So I turned to the pianist, and I noticed he had one finger missing on his right hand. I said, 'can you give me the first words of the song'. The bolshie bastard said, 'I'm here to play for you not to prompt you' and I had to walk off the stage. They paid me off. It was so humiliating; I wanted to crawl into a hole. I didn't want to go home; what was Joe going to say – it was one of his best gigs.

After the disaster at the Osterley, Dorothy had a modicum of success singing with bands and on radio; she'd come to the notice of Charlie Kuntz, an American pianist and band leader, who had his own radio show and he asked her to broadcast with him. The naive Dorothy thought she'd cracked it and only had to sit back and wait for the offers to pour in but it would be four more years before she would broadcast again, this time with another band leader – Billy Reid. Bert and the boys of the Rolling Stones were having tea at Lyon's Corner house, a great meeting place for out of work musicians, when a breathless Dorothy rushed in and excitedly blurted out that she'd got a job; she'd just auditioned at Freeman's rehearsal rooms for Billy Reid.

Billy had been listening to Charlie Kuntz and his band on a late-night BBC radio programme and the vocalist that night just happened to be Dorothy. She had a truly profound effect upon him. So impressed was he by her, that he auditioned her, offered her a better paying job singing with his accordion band and convinced her he could make her a star. The offer was four quid a week but, being more street wise by now, Dorothy haggled and got him to agree to six. Bert told her she was mad, accordion bands were on the way out. 'You can do much better than that Dinah,' he said. 'What about Charlie Kuntz? *He* wants you and he's broadcasting.' 'But I've promised Billy now,' she protested, 'anyway I like him see.' Bert's heart sank; he secretly fancied Dorothy and knew that if she went on tour with the much older and, shall we say more experienced band leader, he wouldn't stand a chance. So, with a heavy heart he wished her luck and calling after her yelled 'keep your hand on your ha'penny Dinah'. 'I will,' she said and with a toss of her head, she was gone.

If she hadn't met Billy things might have been very different. I'm not sure what went on in Chaucer Road, Streatham, but just before Dorothy died she said 'I could have been your mother you know, John'. I don't know if this was a last-minute confession or something she wished had happened – she had always said that *Billy* had taken her virginity on top of a wardrobe skip, backstage in Southampton.

Dorothy was only 16 when she went with Billy; he was twelve years older and married to a dead ringer for the film actress Myrna Loy. Neither fact proved an obstacle to Dorothy's affair with Billy. Dorothy's excuse for breaking up that marriage was, in her words, her extreme youth and naivety. 'Besides,' she said, 'his wife had been away on holiday for eight months.' In the years that followed, Dorothy toured the music halls with Billy's accordion band, honing her stagecraft while Billy, a prolific writer of both music and lyrics, would write songs for her to perform in her own inimitable style.

3

The Composer and the Voice

It was now 1945, pre-television, and radio was the big thing. It could make or break an artist, so you can imagine Dorothy's excitement when she and Billy were spotted by Cecil Madden, the producer of *Variety Bandbox*, the biggest radio show on the air at the time. But Dorothy's excitement was short lived when her performance was cut from the broadcast. She recalled what happened:

> Variety Bandbox was a big troop show. The Beverly sisters did the first one the same time as me. I sang a song of Billy Reid's called 'Safe in My Arms Again'. He'd written the lyrics to a melody that wasn't out of copyright and I was cut out of the broadcast. My mother was ill in hospital at the time. The rest of the family were with her and they all listened. They thought that something had happened to me because I wasn't on. And they [the BBC] tagged … I mean, they put *my* applause, which was fantastic, on the end of the Beverly Sisters' number.

Dorothy played hell, as only Dorothy could, and was given another date. This time she was a big hit and Billy and Dorothy became regulars on the show. The offers came flooding in and they were invited to appear on other shows including Henry Hall's *Guest Night*, another top show of the time. Dorothy's radio appearances became a launching pad for many of her hits, which were penned by Billy. Dorothy had matured by now and was developing into a great hustler. She had meetings with Sir Arthur Lewis, the head of Decca. Sir Arthur took a shine to Dorothy and invited her to a party. She played up to him for all she was worth and successfully pulled off a deal for five of Billy's songs: 'My Mother's Day', 'The Gypsy', 'I'm Walking Behind You', 'I Close My Eyes' and 'Coming Home To You'. The list of songs penned by Billy was endless. All the top artists recorded his songs: Dinah Shaw, The Ink Spots, Eddie Fisher, Louis Armstrong, Pat Boone, Nat King Cole, Bing Crosby, Ella Fitzgerald, Al Jolson, Peggy Lee, Sarah Vaughan, Vera Lynn, Joan Regan, Anne Shelton, David Whitfield, Jimmy Young and last but not least Sinatra himself. Each song had begun its life sung by the inimitable Dorothy Squires.

Billy had five songs in the hit parade on both side of the Atlantic at the same time; a feat not surpassed until the Beatles hit the charts with 'I Want to Hold Your Hand', 'She Loves You', 'Please Please Me', 'Twist and Shout', 'Can't Buy Me Love' and 'Do You Want to Know a Secret'. Billy's royalties must have been enormous. 'The Gypsy', Dorothy's first big hit, would have been the equivalent of a number one in the charts today. But this was 1947 and it wasn't until 1952 that the charts were based on record sales. Back in those days the music market measured a song's popularity by sales of sheet music and the music publishers employed song pluggers to sell their songs.

A song plugger was a vocalist or piano player employed by music publishers to promote and help sell new sheet music, which is how hits were made. They had the unenviable task of trying to get major artists to sing their songs on the radio. Sometimes bribes would be offered called plug money as an inducement but Dorothy was adamant that she never took it: 'Yes I would invite them in and if I could do their song I would. I guess I was the only one that never took plug money from anybody; if they offered me money the bloody song was out.'

Years later, when Dorothy and Billy were topping the bill at the Finsbury Park Empire, a song plugger knocked on her dressing room door and asked if she would sing one of his songs on her radio show. Remembering the slog it had been to get to the top, she was always ready to help the little guy trying to make a buck so she invited him in and asked him to play the song. As he started to play she noticed that he had a part of a finger missing on his left hand. 'Have you ever played at the Osterley Hotel?' she probed. 'Yes,' he said. 'And do you remember a little girl who forgot the words?' 'I don't think I do,' he said. Fixing him with an icy stare she said, 'Well it was me you prick, you refused to give me the first line of my song when I forgot the lyric and I died on my arse – now fuck off.' Dot never forgot a thing; it had taken twenty years but she'd got her own back.

The week Dorothy recorded 'The Gypsy', Dorothy and Billy were topping the bill at the Glasgow Empire. Bert was working the King's Theatre, Edinburgh, so he decided to contact his old friend. Dorothy was over the moon and sent him this letter:

16 Chaucer Rd.
London SE24.
July. Tuesday.

Dear Bert

My goodness fancy hearing from you. How are you man? that's a Welsh phrase as if you didn't know. First let me apologise for my paper. Well Bert, about the Gypsy, it comes out in August, and P.M. publishes it, have I spelt that right? So if you write there they will only be too pleased to forward you a copy on, meanwhile, I will talk to them about it. I am recording it on Thursday for Parlaphone, it comes out in August, I have started recording two months ago, my records are going like hot cakes, thank God as am on Royalties.

I heard about your Brother being killed in the War. I am so very sorry Bert, your mother and Dad must be in an awful state about it. Please convey my deepest sympathy to them both and give them my very best when you write to them.

What are you now doing Bert a single act? We are at the Glasgow Empire for two weeks, starting from next week can you come and have Sunday with us, I may have a few suggestions to see you about. Who do you think is with us this week? Pinky and Margaret, They do a very good act too, they call themselves Lee Brothers and Linda. Very good don't you think? Try and come and see us when you are in Glasgow. You can do it ok? Cheerio for now, give you all the news when we see you.

Lots of good luck
Dinah
x x x x x x x x x x x x x
That's for being so kind to me ten years ago

The next time Bert ran into Dot was at the New Cross Empire in East London. He was doing his band call when he heard a loud raucous woman's voice shouting at the lighting man. 'What the fuck do you think you're doing? Put him in a pink spot,' she yelled. It was Dorothy. She was a big star by now and she thought she was doing Bert a favour but all she was doing was embarrassing him. He dragged her into his dressing room and told her to shut up – she'd get him the sack. 'Never mind that,' she said, 'what do you think of my new tits' and devoid of any false modesty she pulled up her top exposing two very pert breasts.

Dorothy had huge breasts for a little woman – she was only about 5ft 2in and according to her niece, Emily, her tits were 46D. She told me once that if she'd spun around too quickly she would have taken off like a helicopter. The last straw came when she went to Liberty to buy one of their special bras for big-busted women. The assistant, recognising Dorothy, said that she was sorry but they'd put the price up by a pound since last time she'd bought one.

Dorothy flipped, saying that they were expensive enough already 'Fuck it!' she said, 'I'll let them swing first,' and stormed out. On the way home she bumped into Mrs Bemand, the wife of a speciality act she'd worked with called Bemand's Pigeons. Dorothy, still spitting feathers, if you'll excuse the pun, told Mrs Bemand about her altercation with the shop assistant.

Sympathetic to Dorothy's dilemma, Mrs Bemand told her that she knew of a good plastic surgeon that specialised in bust reduction. Dot, never one to do things by halves, decided there and then to have the operation. It was the first cosmetic procedure she had but it certainly wouldn't be the last.

Billy and Dorothy were well and truly in the big time now, topping the bill at every major theatre in the country, billed as the 'Composer and the Voice'. They were earning £10,000 a year, a fortune in 1947. On top of this, Billy's royalties from his writing alone topped £47,000. Whilst Billy and Dot were on tour Dorothy made a discovery that inspired Billy to write one of her biggest hits. They were on their way home from playing the Ardwich Hippodrome in Manchester when the car had a puncture. Fred, Dot's brother, who'd been acting as manager, driver and general gofer, stopped a lorry and went to get help. Dorothy realising she needed a pee, scrambled down a grassy bank to a small cops of trees. It was a lovely moonlit night and Dorothy was awestruck by the beauty of the glade. For all Dot's hard up-front image she was a romantic at heart and cajoled Billy into going back with her to see what she'd found. She recalled:

I wanted to go to have a jimmy riddle [for our American friends it's slang for 'a piddle'] I told Bill, I'm going down there behind those bushes. I went down and there was a stream; not from me I hasten to add. There was a little stream and there was a tree with all hearts and arrows through them; 'I love you' and so on and all the initials carved on them. I was intrigued. It was a beautiful setting. So, I went back up to Bill and as a coincidence, Richard Tauber was singing the song 'Trees' on the car radio. So I said to Bill Reid go down there and see that tree. Well … the next day he wrote 'A Tree in the Meadow' and I launched it at the Brighton Hippodrome with only a piano accompaniment; Bill hadn't had time to write the band parts, and it paralysed them.

Little did she realise then that her wanting to pee would inspire Billy to write a song that would be instrumental in taking her to the USA. It was released in America on the London Label, the American sister to Decca, and Dorothy went to the States to launch it on the *Paul Whiteman Band Show*. As a kid Dorothy had seen a film called *The King of Jazz* six times and the star of that film was Paul Whiteman. Little did she think that years later she would be launching one of Billy Reid's biggest hits on his show at Radio City Music Hall in New York. I can only imagine how she felt, this kid from Llanelli, going to meet the great man. She told me that she was very nervous and didn't know what to call him but he soon put her at her ease: 'What do I call you Mr Whiteman?' she spluttered. 'Call me Pops kid,' he said, 'everybody else does.'

Although Dorothy and Billy's showbiz partnership was a great success, their personal relationship hadn't been an easy ride; Billy had started drinking heavily and was becoming insanely jealous of his much younger lover. He would open her letters and even have her followed. When she got pregnant he accused her of having affairs with members of his band and insisted she have an abortion. I'm not sure how many she had but I gather it was quite a few; something she always regretted in later life because; try as she might, she couldn't carry Roger's to full term. After one of their many rows Billy, trying to make amends, offered to buy Dorothy a mink coat but Dot had other ideas. She'd seen a large Victorian mansion in Bexley village in Kent that had been used as a nursing home. It was for sale for £8,500 and she was determined to get it. She used the £2,500 that Billy had given her for the mink as a deposit and bought St Mary's Mount.

Dot's idea was to turn it into a nightclub. The residents were up in arms; they didn't want showbiz types with their loud music and mad parties ruining their rural idyll. Their protestations were upheld and the application was turned down but Dot had fallen in love with the house so, undeterred, she set about turning it into a palatial Hollywood-style mansion, swimming pool and all. If the neighbours thought that by opposing the application to turn it into a club they would have peace and quiet they had another think coming; Dorothy's extravagant showbiz soirées made more noise than any club would have done.

Dorothy, for all her bravado, missed her family and friends from the old country. So, much to Billy's chagrin, she moved them all in and put them on the payroll. The house became a microcosm of Wales, her Welsh oasis in an English desert. Her father moved into the big house, Rene her sister and Rene's husband George moved into what had been the servants' quarters, Betty, her school friend from Pwll, moved into the lodge with her husband Lee and Dot's brother Fred, who she called Captain Squires after his rank in the army, became her manager. Billy resented this Celtic invasion; the house was always full of Dot's family and friends. Billy had paid for half of the house after all and he felt like an outsider in his own home.

The last nail came in their already rocky relationship when Dorothy, eager for a new project, decided to buy and renovate an old rundown theatre in Llanelli and put on shows. The Astoria had been the cinema where as a starry-eyed kid Dorothy had watched all the Hollywood stars of the day on the silver screen. Little did she imagine that one day she would buy the theatre and show the doubting Thomases of her childhood how successful she'd become:

> The man that owned the theatre was a chemist living next door and he let me have it because he knew me from a kid. Out of five dressing rooms I designed twelve. And I sunk the orchestra pit; the band had to come through the audience. I had them sunk underneath the stage so they walked into the pit. I was a pretty good producer as well, may I say, otherwise I wouldn't have taken on the Palladium.

Dorothy produced and directed many successful variety shows and pantomimes at the theatre, which gave many a performer their start in show business – Leslie Crowther, Morecambe and Wise to name but three. Billy was the musical director and would write all the original music for the shows, one witty lyric being, 'How could Red Riding be good when she's had the wolf at the door'. The opening night at the Astoria was a glittering civic affair with the mayor and mayoress, various councillors and dignitaries and the general glitterati of the town mingling with a number of Dorothy's family and friends.

This was Dorothy's triumphant return to her hometown and she was enjoying every minute of it, strutting about like a peacock, enjoying the plaudits of the crowd. The family was getting stuck into the hors d'oeuvres as if they hadn't seen food for a week when Billy entered with another woman on his arm. He'd had a few too many and announced in a very loud voice that the lady with him was his wife. Dorothy was very embarrassed. She'd been living with Billy as man and wife for eleven years and, as far as the public was concerned, they were a married couple, although, he hadn't been entirely faithful to her; he'd been shagging a member of a girl group in her show called the Copper Knobs. Mrs Reid sarcastically suggested to Dorothy that she should marry Billy as *she* didn't want him anymore, to which Dorothy replied, 'You're eleven years too fucking late love.' Billy, incensed by this, yelled that she had no right to speak to his wife like that. Dorothy retaliating said, she'd speak to her any way she liked in her own theatre and how dare he humiliate her in front of her family. Billy completely lost it, 'Don't you think I had something to do with it?' he yelled. 'And as for your bloody family; I've been a human cornucopia to your fucking family; they're nothing but a lot of freeloading bastards and thieves … I've been keeping the fuckers for years.'

With that all hell broke loose. Dorothy smacked Billy across the face. He made a grab for her, Dorothy's father tried to grab Billy, the front of house manager intervened, Billy pushed him and he fell on top of Dorothy's father, who then made a grab for the mayor to save himself and knocked him to the ground. It was like the Keystone Cops. 'That's it,' Dorothy screamed, 'I've had it with you. I've put up with your insults and insinuations for long enough.' Then, turning to Billy's wife screamed: 'You can have him love; as far as I'm concerned, as of now we're through – over and fucking out!!'

For all Dorothy's protestations, Billy still owned half of the theatre and to add insult to injury he employed his wife to work in the box office. I'm not sure how long Dorothy suffered this humiliating situation but the relationship was on a downward spiral from there on in and ended very acrimoniously. I asked her when the final split came:

My break with Bill started through the theatre in Llanelli. It wasn't my doing it was just one of those things. We were ready for splitting long before I met Roger Moore. He was a Libran. Bill was a Libran; I'm cursed with Librans. My sister's one, my niece is one, everyone I know was a Libran and they all have the same characteristics. I'm an Aries. Anyhow, enough of that; I'm trying to get the continuity of this now … Bill Reid was drinking very heavily; I suppose it was understandable, he had five hits in the hit parade and the pressure got to him and apart from which I was having tremendous success, if you know what I mean! We were playing the Empress Brixton and I was ready to go on. My sister was dressing me at this particular time and the zip went in my dress and I had to go back and change it. We were on the end of it then [the relationship], Billy Reid was so jealous, and I never gave him cause. Jealous! I couldn't talk to anybody; he'd have me followed. This particular night when I got my dress changed, he was just about to introduce me and when I went on I could see him gesturing to the audience as if I had been drinking. I'd never been drunk on stage in my life. Faith Brown did an impersonation of me in her act once, walking about the stage with a glass of booze in her hand. Can you imagine me being on the stage for two and a half hours and not forgetting anecdotes that I had to place and remembering every line of the songs? But what could I do? Urban myths stick and I was fed up with having to deny it so in the end I just gave up. When I saw Billy intimating that I was pissed, I decided that that was the last show I would ever do with him. When the curtain came down, he used to hold the curtain for me, I didn't go through. That was it. What I saw him do to the audience, that was the finish of him there and then. If I'd have deserved it I wouldn't have cared but I didn't.

After the split Billy went back to the Isle of Wight and continued to write songs while Dorothy remained cocooned in her great mansion in Bexley with her family and concentrated on a solo career. It must have been a strange experience going it alone. The stage must have felt a lonely place without Billy by her side; he'd been with her, as both lover and mentor, throughout her professional career. But Dorothy soldiered on and it wasn't long before she had another hit, ironically a song written by Billy. He'd written 'I'm Walking Behind You' on finding that the girl he had loved for twelve years had replaced him with the younger and more handsome Roger and his sadness is reflected in this simple poignant lyric:

I'm walking behind you, on your wedding day,
I hear you promise, to love and obey,
Though you may forget me, you're still on my mind,
Look over your shoulder, I'm walking behind,
Maybe I'll kiss again, with a love that's new,
But I shall wish again, I was kissing you,
'Cos I'll always love you, wherever you go,
And though we are parted, I want you to know,
That if things go wrong, dear, and fate is unkind
Look over your shoulder, I'm walking behind.

4

The Roger Years

It was through Dorothy's predilection for throwing big parties that Roger Moore entered her life. Roger was just a struggling actor and part-time knitwear model for *Woman's Own* when he met Dorothy. He was doing a small part in a film when he befriended Dorothy's old school friend, Betty Newman, who'd been an extra on the same film. Boop, as Betty was affectionately known, asked Roger if he would like to go to a party at Dorothy's house. I'm sure Roger had heard of Dot's parties, and never one to turn down an invitation to a social event that could perhaps further his career he said he would. Having been to many of Dot's parties, I can imagine what it must have been like. The enormous pile that was St Mary's Mount would have been alive with people – an incongruous mix of prize fighters, builders, actors, musicians, producers and record bosses. Her parties looked like scenes from a Hollywood movie. A pianist would have been tinkling a white grand piano in the background with Dorothy singing or holding court, her language ripe as usual. Not being there that night, I can only relay what Dorothy told me about that first meeting:

When Roger arrived at Bexley railway station he called the house and told me that Betty had invited him to the party and asked how could he find St Mary's Mount. I told him to wait at the station and I would send someone to get him. I asked him how the driver would recognise him. Ever the joker, Roger said that he was short fat and bald.

When Roger made his entrance it was obvious that he was anything but short fat and bald and Dorothy was immediately attracted to him. I'm sure the feeling was mutual for although Dorothy was twelve years older than Roger, at 36 she was still in her prime and a very charismatic woman; she wasn't just a star, she had the aura of stardom; when she walked into the room, she lit it up. Dorothy had two personalities – the down to earth Welsh woman that her friends saw and the up-front professional persona for the public. The only time I ever saw her drop her guard was when she was around someone she fancied; she became, for want of a better word, coquettish.

The night she met Roger she was being very coquettish; she fancied him but she was trying very hard to play it cool. Dorothy always insisted on doing all the cooking for her parties and her barbecue chicken was to die for. She was throwing pieces of chicken onto two huge solid silver trays and smothering them in barbeque sauce when Roger followed her into the kitchen and, in her words, was hovering. Dorothy, not wanting to look too keen, told him she was busy but if he wanted another drink to help himself. 'No thanks,' he said, 'I've got an ulcer but they are fashionable aren't they!' 'Who writes your fucking scripts?' she quipped. 'Hollywood's finest, hopefully,' he countered.

Later, when the party was coming to an end and most of the guests had gone, Roger was still hanging back, hovering, poking the dying embers of the fire and making no attempt to go. Dorothy told him that her maid's son could give him a lift to the station. Stalling for time, he said he thought the last train had gone. Roger, captivated by the charismatic Dorothy, suddenly kissed her. Dorothy, taken aback, asked what the fuck he thought he was doing. Ignoring her protestations, he picked her up in his arms and carried her up the grand sweeping staircase. She said she felt like Vivien Leigh in

Gone with the Wind and from that moment on it was obvious that he would become the love of her life.

There is no doubt that Dorothy was in love with Roger but she was well aware of the age gap and would do anything to please him. When Roger, on seeing her walk up the stairs one night, criticised her legs she started working out with an almost maniacal ferocity in order to please her younger lover. It was an unfounded accusation I might add – she had great legs. Their relationship wasn't always a bed of roses. Mary, the maid told me that she would often come in to clean and find the best Royal Dalton china smashed all over the kitchen floor where Dorothy had been throwing it at Roger. Roger was still married to his first wife, Doorn Van Steyn, at this time and Dorothy wasn't too pleased when she found out he'd been going back to see her. He tried to explain to Dorothy that it was only because he wanted to talk Doorn out of naming her in the divorce but Dot wasn't having any of it. She called him a fucking liar then, flinging a national paper in his face and screaming 'It didn't fucking work then did it?' Her name was splashed all over the front page, naming her as co-respondent. It is alleged that Doorn claimed that Roger had promised to come back to her but she sent him packing and later wrote a book called *A Saint He Aint*, which to this day has never been published – I wonder why?

For all their arguments, Dorothy was besotted with Roger but they were often apart. Dot's solo career had taken off and whilst she was on tour playing to packed houses all over the country, Roger had to be content with small parts and £8-a-time modelling jobs just to keep body and soul together. Dorothy, being smitten with her new beau, took every opportunity to rush back to Bexley so they could be together. The situation wasn't ideal so Dorothy suggested that he go on tour with her – he could be the master of ceremonies for her show. He protested that he wasn't a *turn*. But Dorothy, who wasn't about to take no for an answer, cajoled that if he were the MC for the show they could be together. So Roger, having nothing better to do, capitulated and joined the tour.

Although he was a bit of a raconteur, his jokes being a big hit amongst friends and family, he soon found out that it was a very different story performing to an audience who'd paid for their tickets. His jokes about parrots fell flat and he died on his arse. One of the tour dates was the Pontypridd Town Hall. Bert was back in Wales by this time and went backstage to see his old friend. He wasn't too impressed with Roger's performance and asked Dot who the bum MC was. 'Shut up,' she said, 'I'm going to marry him.' Bert was gobsmacked. 'Are you nuts,' he said, 'it'll never last, he only looks about twelve.' But it did last – eight years to be exact.

Roger and Dorothy had been together for seven of those years when Billy Reid came out of the woodwork. On 14 March 1958 he took Dorothy to court, claiming that he and Dorothy held equal shares in St Mary's Mount and its contents. He was seeking an injunction restraining her from disposing of them without his consent. The break up with Billy had been described as a catalogue of tears and fisticuffs in a seemingly endless round of court cases. The following is a blow-by-blow account of the final case.

Billy claimed that he had lived with Dorothy as man and wife from 1939 to 1950 sharing equally the money they received, from their stage partnership, except for his royalties. He told the court that they each paid half the purchase price of the house, bought in 1948 for £8,600 and he also paid for half the furniture. Responding to her council, Dorothy told the court that Billy used to drink excessively. The council then asked her if this affected her happiness. 'Very much so,' she replied. 'He used to hit me in front of people and humiliate me.' Dorothy broke down in the witness box under cross-examination and watched by a crowded courtroom asked permission to take some tablets. Justice Vaisey gave his permission and Dorothy took two tablets from her handbag, dissolved them in a glass of water and drank the mixture down in one gulp. Regaining her composure, she told the court of the final scene that ended in their parting:

It was in Jan 1951 after the show, I was standing at the bar of my theatre in Llanelli with the mayor and a bank manager and other people that I won't mention when he, Billy Reid, came in and twisted my arm round. He said, 'You think you are the bloody owner of this theatre don't you!' I told him not to act like this in front of all these people in the bar. Then a fight broke out; there was so much scrapping going on. It was shocking. My father tried to stop it but he ended up on the floor.

The judge then asked her how he ended up on the floor. She told him that she didn't remember, there was so much going on. The judge commented that it sounded like a very confused scene to him and asked if they were all sober. Dorothy replied that *she* was perfectly sober – she was on a diet. Then shooting a glance at Billy, said that she couldn't speak for the others. Carrying on, she claimed that she bought St Mary's Mount in her own name and with her own money. She used the £2,500, which Billy had given her to buy a mink coat for the deposit for the house. She also counterclaimed for £3,000 that she said was a half share she had spent in connection with their stage act and for £169, which she said she had spent on Mr Reid's behalf.

Dorothy and Billy both had their claims against each other dismissed with costs in the High Court. Mr Justice Vaisey advised them to call it quits saying that, 'The lady is still heard and listened to and it may be that the best thing is to call it quits and get on with life'. 'I can only hope,' he continued, 'that the result of this action may restore some measure of amity between you and you can serve the public by the exercise of your talents and your skills.'

Summing up, Mr Justice Vaisey judged that Dorothy could have the house but would lose the counter claim. 'Mr Reid has not established his claim to the house but has defeated Miss Squires on her counterclaim.' The judge went on to say that he thought that the task of cleaning up the affairs of a partnership would be almost impossible and he did not recommend that any more money and time be spent on it adding, that in his opinion:

The house was bought for the primary object of giving Miss Squires a home. Mr Reid had provided part of the purchase price but it was put into her name with the genuine and honest intention that it should be hers out and out, and that if Mr Reid were to go bankrupt he could say truthfully that the house was hers.

It was a bittersweet victory – Dorothy had won the legal battle but not the moral one. She would often say when anything went wrong in her life, 'It's the man upstairs paying me back for what I did to Billy Reid.' After the break-up Billy married Jane Gordon, another Welsh singer with whom he tried to revive his flagging stage and recording career, but the dizzy heights he'd reached with Dorothy were never to be realised and the huge amount he'd earned as 'The Composer and the Voice' was soon depleted. He sold his royalties to make ends meet and to this day they remain in someone else's hands, with his descendants not receiving a penny. Sadly he was made bankrupt, retired from show business and died almost penniless on the Isle of Wight.

5

A Solo Career

Although Dorothy had broken up with Billy she was still in demand as a recording artist. Dorothy was always a good judge of a song and knew a hit as soon as she heard it. She wanted to record 'I'm Walking Behind You' but her A&R man Ray Martin didn't like it and was refusing to record it. He told Dorothy that it was his job to find material for her to record and as she was contracted to Columbia she had no option but to do as he said. Maddened by his response, she went looking for the contract to see if there was any way she could get out of it. She searched everywhere and eventually found it in an unopened envelope on the mantelpiece – her maid had forgotten to post it. Fortuitously she wasn't signed to Columbia after all.

Still determined to record 'I'm Walking Behind You', she decided to go it alone, hiring the studio and paying for the session herself. Allan Freeman, her recording manager and Jimmy Phillips the publisher, weren't sure it was worth recording either as Eddie Fisher, father of Carrie Fisher and third husband of Elizabeth Taylor, had turned it down in the States. Dorothy was adamant, if she didn't know a hit song by now, she never would and why were they worried anyway – 'she was paying for the fucking session, not them!'

After the session Jimmy Phillips asked if he could have an acetate copy of the recording, explaining that it was for the song pluggers to promote it. Dorothy thought the request was a bit odd but agreed. She should have gone with her first instinct; Jimmy sent it to the States and Eddie Fisher being impressed by Dorothy's recording changed his mind and recorded it too. Eddie Fisher was one of the top singing stars at the time and his version went straight into the American charts.

When Dorothy found out she was as mad as hell and decided to fly to the States to confront James Franks, president of Coral Records, face to face. By now Roger was getting more and more frustrated with the way his career was going; he didn't seem to be getting anywhere and confided in Dot that he didn't think that he would ever make it. 'Let's face it,' he said, 'I'm not the greatest actor in the world.' 'Since when did you have to be a good actor to become a film star?' she quipped. 'Anyway, what are you worried about, you're living in the lap of luxury, not like most struggling actors.' Dorothy suggested he go with her to the States. It made sense; she had contacts there and could ring a few friends to see if she could get something going for him. 'You'll stand a better chance in America,' she said, 'because unless you're an ugly bastard with one ear in this country you don't stand a chance – and ugly may I say, you aint.' So, in 1953 a happier and more optimistic Roger and Dorothy set sail on the *Queen Mary* bound for New York.

On arrival Dorothy went to Coral Records and demanded to see James Franks, the president of the company. Ignoring the secretary's protestations Dorothy, all 5ft 2in of her, exploded into the office demanding attention. Standing, hands on hips in front of James Franks she said, 'Okay Jimmy Jesus, why has Eddie Fisher covered my record? Why did he change his mind all of a fuckin' sudden? I thought he hated the song.' James Franks, trying to diffuse the situation told Dorothy, as diplomatically as he could, that she didn't have an exclusive on the song and that Eddie had heard her acetate and liked it. Dorothy hit the roof 'What do you mean *my* acetate?' she screamed, 'Those bastards in England had no right to send the acetate without my permission.'

If they thought Dorothy was going take this lying down, they were mistaken; she wasn't going to give up on this one. She was up against it though; all the major stations in the States were pushing the Eddie Fisher version but Dorothy was determined. She decided to go on the road to plug it on all the local radio stations. If she could cover enough of them it was as good as having a network play. She travelled miles in her quest but even the incorrigible Dorothy had to admit defeat in the end. Her foray into the song pluggers' world hadn't paid off and she had to settle for just the UK hit. Dorothy decided to stay in the States for a while. She set up temporary home with Roger in the exclusive Park Chambers in Manhattan and embarked on an almost blinkered obsessional quest to make him a star:

> It took time for Roger to break into film; people say it was my influence; that I made Roger a star. It's become a bit of an urban myth and, undoubtedly my contacts pushed him in the right direction but I could only open doors for him, he had to walk through them. So, hand on heart I can't take all the credit.

Dorothy contacted her old friend Charles Coburn. Dot told me he had a bit of a crush on her and even suggested that she divorce Roger and marry him:

> I knew there were always plenty of beautiful girls hanging around Roger. Not that I fell short! Charles Coburn, he was a big star, he used to say 'Why don't you divorce Roger and marry me?' I used to say 'Why don't you marry Blanch Sweet?' She was big too, big name, apparently – and he said – [she pauses] No, I won't say it or you'll be cross; anyway, OK ... He said 'Why should I marry any of 'em when I can fuck 'em all?'

Using Charles' infatuation to her full advantage, she told him that she was trying to get something going for Roger in the States and would appreciate it if he could point her in the right direction. Charles had lots of contacts amongst the Hollywood set and invited Dorothy and Roger to a party at the Plaza Hotel that was being thrown for Mary Martin by Hedda Hopper, the famous gossip columnist.

It was a typical showbiz bash where cigar-smoking agent types were mingling with well-known stars of the day: Gary Cooper, Shirley McLane,

Grace Kelly, Doris Day, Rock Hudson and Angie Dickinson et al. It was like the who's who of Hollywood. Dorothy was mingling with the cream of showbiz society and she loved it. She seemed to have forgotten Roger, who was trailing behind her like a lost dog. Charles introduced Dorothy to Bill David, a radio station manager, explaining that she was over to promote her new record. Bill said he had seen Dot on the *Paul Whiteman Show* and said he loved her version of 'I'm Walking Behind You' but it was a pity that the major stations were going with the Eddie Fisher cut. He offered to give Dot some airtime though, saying he would do anything for a Brit, as his wife was one. It was a fortuitous meeting for Roger because as luck would have it, Bill David's wife was a theatrical producer called Nancy David and she just happened to be looking for an English actor for a play she was producing. Bill explained that it was too expensive to bring one over from England and asked Dorothy if she knew of any cheap English actors. Dorothy, tongue in cheek, said she might know of one.

The next day Dorothy, putting on her best managerial voice, called Nancy David, told her that she'd heard that she was looking for an English actor for her forthcoming play and it so happened that she was representing an actor called Roger Moore. A meeting was set up, a deal was done and Roger got the job. It wasn't the break Roger had hoped for though; the play was a real turkey – it opened and closed the same night. The notices the next day were disastrous. A critic from the *Hollywood Reporter* wrote: '*Pin to See a Peep Show* was a glum hackneyed cockney piece – our cousins across the water usually have a stylish way with murder, but I'm afraid the conclusion about this one is dial M for Boredom.'

By now Dorothy was running out of cash, they'd been in the States for some time and it had been an expensive business socialising, trying to promote Roger's career. Dorothy was still in demand as a performer in England so she decided to go home to earn some more money. Roger tried to persuade her not to go, he was afraid she wouldn't come back. 'Why wouldn't I come back,' she said, 'I think I'm pregnant.' Unfortunately, Dorothy lost her longed for child. She'd had a number of miscarriages during her marriage to Roger and never did realise her dream of becoming a mother. It was one of her biggest regrets in life. Ironically, after having had several abortions with Billy Reid, she couldn't carry Roger's to full term. She would often say: 'I had my legs in the air for seven years for that bastard and still couldn't keep them.'

Dorothy told me of one incident when she and Roger were driving back from the studio in Los Angeles. Roger had to slam on the breaks, to avoid a truck, which gave her a jolt and she later miscarried. On another occasion, Hilda Brown, Dorothy's secretary, told me that she was in Dot's dressing room at the Talk of the Town when she started to miscarry. The room was full of flowers and good luck messages, the simpering sycophants and freeloaders were playing to Dot's ego. Hilda was handing around the hors d'oeuvres and champagne when Dorothy was suddenly struck by a bad twinge of stomach ache. She doubled up in agony. Hilda, being concerned, ushered the hangers-on out of the dressing room then, slinging Dorothy's fur coat over her shoulders, took her home. Needless to say she lost yet another baby. It was becoming a regular occurrence and Dorothy had to face the agonising fact that she would never have the one thing in her life that she longed for – to become a mother. She swore it was Roger's fault. She even sent him to a doctor for tests. He came back with what he called his baby pills but it didn't make any difference. It was obvious that it wasn't Roger's fertility that was in question, as later he would father three healthy children but to Dorothy's sorrow not with her.

I'm not sure if it was Roger's idea or Dorothy's but they decided to get married before she returned to England. The $25 wedding ceremony was held at the courthouse in New Jersey on 6 June 1953. It was witnessed by Warren, Latona and Sparks – a knockabout comedy act who had supported Dorothy on the Moss Empire circuit and Joe Latona, a member of the group, was the best man. The small reception that followed at Jack Dempsey's Club was a meagre affair. They didn't even have any wedding photos to remember the day – Dorothy had left her new shoes at the courthouse and Roger had to rush back to get them and consequently missed the photo shoot. On the morning of the wedding Roger wanted to make love but Dot, being very superstitious, thought it was unlucky. Roger was very persuasive though so Dorothy, putting her superstitions aside for once, made passionate love with her husband to be, resulting in her arriving for the ceremony looking rather flushed. Perhaps Dot was right to be superstitious; the marriage she thought would last forever hadn't got off to a good start and was soon destined to run into troubled waters.

Dorothy flew back to England to fulfil TV and film commitments and earn some much needed funds; Roger had been out of work for some time and the cost of trying to promote his career had been enormous; she told me that on the day of the wedding she only had $12 left in her pocket. When she arrived back in England, Dorothy threw herself into learning the part for her first acting role in a film called *Stars in Your Eyes*. She'd been performing since she was a kid but, apart from pantomime and a few odd sketches in *Summer Season*, Dorothy hadn't acted before. But she had a way with words; anyone who saw her sell a song could see she believed every word of the text; she wasn't known as the method singer for nothing and acting for her was a natural progression.

She loved working with her old friend Nat Jackley but didn't get on very well with the star of the film, Pat Kirkwood. On the other hand, with the co-star, Bonar Colleano, she hit it off immediately. She recalled that, 'he used to get a hard-on every time we went into a clinch.' When the wrap came Dorothy cabled her $1,500 fee to her joint account in America to keep things going for Roger until she got back. On returning to the States, she and Roger moved to Hollywood and set up home in Westwood Village. It was the happiest she'd ever been; she got to see America with the man she loved and with whom she thought loved her. For the first time in her life there was a career far more important than hers; she was content to be a housewife, read cookbooks, study music and do a little writing while Roger concentrated on his career.

After a number of forgettable films, the most forgettable being *Diane* with Lana Turner, Roger's five-year contract with MGM came to an ignominious end; he was sacked with still three years to go. Dorothy and Roger decided to return to England where Dorothy was still in demand as a performer. Dorothy's film *Stars in Your Eyes* coincidentally had its London premiere at the same time that Roger signed a new contract with Columbia to film

Ivanhoe, a series to be filmed mainly in England. Dorothy, never one to miss an opportunity, suggested that she and Roger write a title song for the series. It was written for a male singer but when they couldn't find a suitable candidate Dorothy stepped up and, in her own words, 'Sang her balls off.' Unfortunately it wasn't chosen to be the theme and although Dorothy wrote over 156 songs during her career it wasn't until a few years later that she had real success with a film theme – the aforementioned *Tammy Tell Me True*. In those days actors looked upon TV work as second class and Roger had always aspired to be a film star so when he was offered a film by Warner Brothers, based on a stage play called *The Miracle*, he jumped at it and Dorothy and Roger were on their way back to Hollywood. But the tenacious Dorothy continued to haggle for Roger behind the scenes:

> An executive from Warner's rang and I answered the phone. He asked me if I was looking forward to Roger being on board. I said yes, but not at these prices I told Warner Brothers, I said 'he's just finished a big TV series and you'll have to pay for that: Fifteen hundred dollars a week, and don't give me that rubbish about keeping him on a salary for just forty weeks of the year either!' and Roger became the highest paid contract artist for Warner Brothers.

Dorothy was well aware of beautiful girls hanging around the film sets and Roger, by his own admission, was a bit of a lothario. He used to say that a man's prick was like a 'divining rod that found trouble for men' – it certainly found trouble for *him* when he started an affair with Dorothy Provine, his leading lady in *The Alaskans*. Dorothy never went with Roger when he was on set; she didn't think it right. When I asked her if she was jealous of the girls hanging around, feigning false bravado, she said, 'a shag to a man is like taking a crap he's forgotten it straight after.' She may have believed that but Roger's affair with Provine really hit her hard; she descended into deep depression and lost 3 stone in weight. When someone asked her what diet she was on she quipped sardonically, 'My husband having an affair diet.' Dorothy had heard rumours that Roger was having an affair of course but couldn't prove it until one night when Roger started talking in his sleep:

I was next to him. The sound of his deep breathing, and snoring was disturbing me so I poked him in the back. Roger groaned and turned over without waking. He mumbled something incoherent; I put it down to a dreaming man's wanderings at first. Then, quite audibly, he sighed 'Oh … Dorothy.' When I confronted him the next morning, he feigned innocence as usual and asked me what the hell I was talking about. 'Dorothy fucking Provine,' I said, 'you're poking her aren't you! You've been calling her name out in your sleep.' He said, 'But your name is Dorothy.' 'Yes,' I said, 'but you always call me *Dot* you fucking whoremaster.'

Roger couldn't see what all the fuss was about, to him Dorothy Provine was just a bit of fun but to Dorothy it was a major tragedy. There were the usual histrionics, smashing of china etc. When he came home from filming a little worse for wear he found that Dorothy had locked him out. Mad as hell, he threw all the loungers into the swimming pool. Then, having got it out of his system, he wrapped himself in his overcoat and settled down to sleep on the deck. Eventually Dorothy let him in and things seemed to go back to normal for a while but it was one more nail in an already half-nailed coffin. After confronting Roger about his infidelity, Dorothy returned to England to fulfil some cabaret engagements, which gave Roger some space and Dot time to calm down. When she eventually flew back to Los Angeles, Billy Marsh, her agent from the Bernard Delfont Organisation, accompanied her.

One Sunday night Roger, Dorothy and Billy decided to go to see the controversial comedian Lenny Bruce. The audience were enjoying his risqué act when all hell broke loose; Mr Bruce had made a negative remark about the London Palladium. That was it – Dorothy, who having had a few too many yelled, 'You'd like the fucking chance to play there, you no talent prick.' Bruce hit back with a one liner and Dorothy countered with 'fuck you.' A few people around the table were starting to look at them by now and Roger was embarrassed. He called for the bill then, draping Dot's mink coat over her shoulders, tried to drag her out, apologising as he went. This didn't stop her tirade. 'You couldn't get arrested in England,' she screeched, 'we've got comics there that would fucking lose you.' All the audience were staring by this time and Dorothy, noticing their stares, yelled over her shoulder: 'What you all looking at? I'm a fucking star in England!' The writing was on the wall for this ill-fated marriage and it was never more apparent than when Dorothy attended a preview with Roger for his first Hollywood film. Although Dorothy was glad that Roger had made it, paradoxically it stuck in her craw that his career had eclipsed hers. She was still in her prime and a damn good performer to boot, and for all her protestations that she was happy to be a housewife nothing could have been further from the truth.

Although the marriage was beginning to show the cracks, they still kept up appearances at social events, one of which was the launch of a film Roger had done with Elizabeth Taylor called *The Last Time I Saw Paris*. It was a glitzy affair at a movie theatre on Olympic Boulevard. The cast list of names read like a who's who of Hollywood: Elizabeth Taylor, Van Johnson, Donna Reed, Walter Pigeon, Eva Gabor, George Dolenz and Roger of course; he'd made it onto the big screen in Hollywood. They arrived in a limo at the theatre. He was dressed in black tie, Dorothy, in a very expensive looking gown. Dorothy was all smiles, basking in Roger's reflected glory. She swept into the foyer followed by Roger and by her attitude you would think it was *her* event not his. But Roger was the centre of attention now and it was her turn to feel like the second banana and she didn't like it; in Britain she was 'Dorothy Squires not Mrs Roger Bloody Moore'. On a subsequent occasion Roger and Dorothy were invited to a small dinner party being held for Gloria Swanson, who arrived elegantly attired in a black velvet gown with just a diamond clip at her throat. Dorothy was sat next to Butler Mills, boss of the Alka Seltzer Company who introduced her to Frank Sennett, the owner of the Moulin Rouge, a large nightclub in Hollywood. This turned out to be a fortuitous meeting – ironically, not for Roger but this time for Dorothy.

Butler Mills, like most people, was captivated by Dot's personality and asked her if she would like to work in the States. She said she would love to but she wasn't too pleased when he suggested that she would have to audition. She said she hadn't auditioned since 1933 and she wasn't about to start now. After a bit of haggling a deal was struck for Dot to do a Sunday show for $250 expenses with a view to a longer contract. He asked her if she was used to big rooms in England. 'Is the London Palladium big enough for you?' she quipped. What she didn't tell him was that the last time she'd appeared on the Palladium she'd taken over the top of the bill spot from Two Ton Tessie O'Shea, who'd fallen off an elephant. It was 1946 in a revue called *High Time*. Tessie made her appearance on the back of an elephant – an impressive entrance spoiled somewhat by the elephant being pregnant. Tessie's ample frame proved just too much for Jumbo to bear and she threw her off; she was out of the show for three months. Dorothy took over the reins, not of the elephant I might add. Anyway, back to the plot. The night came when Dorothy was to appear at the Moulin Rouge in Hollywood. Her dressing room was full of English expats. Her old friend, Charles Coburn, arrived with Sir Cedric Hardwicke bearing two-dozen red roses; Charles Laughton and Trevor Howard were also there. Trevor Howard introduced Laughton to Dorothy saying that she was a great artist. Laughton, who was three sheets to the wind, said he'd seen all her paintings to which Howard quipped, 'she's a singer you twat.'

One of her biggest fans was a young Elvis Presley, who was virtually unknown at the time. He went to most of her performances just to hear her sing 'This is My Mother's Day'. After her first performance he went backstage and nervously introduced himself. Elvis told Dot how much he admired her and hoped he might have just a little of the success she had achieved. If only she knew what an icon he would become. When hearing of The King's sad demise, Dorothy's proud if somewhat egotistical response was, 'Poor Elvis, he was my biggest fan.'

Dorothy's opening night was a triumph; she took the LA audience by storm. After the show, Frank Sennett came backstage and asked her if she would consider staying on for an extra month as the headliner. Dorothy full of her Celtic charm said, 'Are you fucking kidding – you just try and stop me.' The next day there were huge posters displaying Dorothy's picture all over Hollywood. Dorothy told me that she drove around the block a dozen times just to see the life-size posters of herself smiling down from the giant hoardings. At the end of her run, Sennett approached Dorothy and offered her a season at the Desert Inn in Las Vegas, supporting the great Schnozzle

Durante, for a fee of $50,000. Incredibly, she turned it down. Dorothy was desperately trying to have a baby with Roger at the time and she didn't want to take a chance on anything going wrong – she'd had two miscarriages already and her body clock was ticking. Try as he might Sennett couldn't persuade her to sign the contract. He wasn't used to being turned down and fell out with her big time and refused to take any of her calls. Ironically, Dorothy lost the baby *and* the chance to appear in Vegas – another sacrifice she'd made for love.

This wouldn't be the last offer for her to work in the States; she'd gone to see Edith Piaf perform in Hollywood with her American agent Elgin, who was the American representative for the Grade Organisation and the booker of the Fontenblue Hotel in Miami. Piaf was magic. Dot was so moved by her performance that she went backstage to meet her. Piaf told Dorothy, in her broken English, that she'd loved Dot's arrangement of her song, 'Hymne L'Amour'. Dorothy had recorded the English version called 'If You Love Me' and Piaf was raving about it in front of the booker. The next morning Dorothy received a call offering her to go into a revue at the Fontainebleau. But again she turned it down, saying she was still trying for a baby. Another offer she rejected was to join the Andrew Sisters, a very successful American close harmony group of the swing and Boogie-woogie era, who sold nearly a million records during their career. They were three sisters: La Verne, Maxine and Patty. When Patty Andrews died Dorothy, having the same range as Patty, was asked to join them. She considered it for a while, even flying to the States to discuss becoming a member of the famous trio but true to form she turned the contract down.

She continued to turn offer after offer down in her quest to become a mother – even refusing an offer from Sir Cameron Macintosh to replace Dolores Grey in *Follies*. Although Dorothy was a brilliant performer, she was an individual; I don't think she could have taken direction from anyone. I can just imagine if she had done *Follies*; on the opening night she would have ignored the stage direction, come down stage and started to belt it out, upstaging the rest of the cast. I'm sure it would have been a great career move and lots of stars would have jumped at the chance, but Dorothy was adamant:

'What would my fans think of me just singing one song? Besides, they only offered me £1,500 quid a week; I'm worth more than that.'

But probably one of the biggest mistakes of her career was when she turned down the William Morris Agency, the biggest theatrical agency in the States at the time. After her success at the Moulin Rouge, she was approached by the agency as they wanted to represent her. She would have been in good company; as they also handled such luminaries as Clark Gable, Judy Garland, Bill Cosby, Katherine Hepburn, Jack Lemon, Walter Matthau, Marilyn Monroe, Sammy Davis and Frank Sinatra; the list was endless. The agency was a powerhouse and could have made Dorothy a huge star in the States but her single-mindedness, or should I say bloody-mindedness, lost her the chance of a lifetime. After endless negotiations she refused to sign, her excuse being that she had too many commitments at home in England. The real truth was Roger's philandering with Dorothy Provine had taken its toll and she kept returning home to Britain to find comfort amongst her family and friends. The agency, feeling that they couldn't rely on her, withdrew their offer and even threatened to blacklist her to other agents. And so Dorothy closed at the Moulin Rouge on the Saturday and flew home to England on the Sunday.

Dot's marriage was pretty much on the rocks by this time and rumours abounded in the press of a break-up. On her arrival in London the awaiting flock of paparazzi swooped and pecked. Dorothy fended them off, vehemently denying rumours of a break-up, saying: 'It's only one of Roger's little jokes … he's always making jokes.' Dorothy told me that Roger's excuse for his affair with Dorothy Provine had been because he'd been depressed by the lack of any decent film offers but rumour had it that he'd actually fallen for the pretty blond actress. Dorothy dealt with the situation the only way she knew how by going back to work, but there wasn't much call for torch singers like Dorothy in the late fifties. Rock 'n' roll had crossed the Atlantic, variety was on its last legs and the promoters had to put pop singers of the day on the bill to bring in the younger crowds.

Dorothy was booked to appear in a variety show at the London Hippodrome but when she arrived at the theatre she found that Charlie

Gracie, an American rock 'n' roll singer was top of the bill. She blew her top. The manager tried to calm her down but she wasn't having any of it. 'I've just arrived from a big success in Hollywood,' she yelled, 'And I was promised equal top billing not first featured artist.' The manager protested that it wasn't down to him; she would have to take it up with her agent. 'You can fucking bet on it,' she screamed and stormed out. By this time punters were gathering in the foyer to book tickets, some of whom were Dorothy's fans, and they weren't too pleased when they found out she would not be appearing. Ironically, Charlie Gracie, who's become a friend of late, told me that his son is one of Dorothy's biggest fans.

After Roger's ineffective foray into film, he'd been let go by MGM and signed as a contract actor by Warner Brothers. After a few uninspiring roles, in equally uninspiring films, it was obvious that Jack Warner didn't see Roger as a leading man and he was transferred to Warner Brothers Television. Roger had always aspired to be a film star and was really pissed off. It seemed that he had blown it in Hollywood so reluctantly he followed Dorothy back to England and changed his agent, signing with the Lew and Leslie Grade Organisation, who ironically were Dorothy's agents at the time. The only films he was being offered by his new agents came from Italian and French companies that made cut-price Spaghetti Westerns. A script that came through the door called *Rape of the Sabine Women* didn't fill him with enthusiasm but Dorothy reminded him that he'd left Hollywood because he hated television and cajoled that at least it was a film offer. So Roger accepted it and left for Rome. That film would have life-changing consequences for Dorothy and Roger. Dorothy had opted to stay in England to promote her latest record, 'Say It With Flowers', rather than go with Roger to Rome – a decision she lived to regret for the rest of her life. She never did see that picture or Rome and Roger never again returned to the marital bed.

I suppose the up side to all this, if you can call it an up side, was that 'Say It With Flowers,' a song she recorded with her old friend Russ Conway, became another of Dorothy's big hits. Russ had been visiting Dorothy in America with his recording manager, Norman Newell, when Russ discovered that fateful song. It had lain largely forgotten gathering dust in her piano stool when Russ, while looking through some manuscripts, came across a handwritten copy of it. He played it, liked it and Norman had the brainwave for Russ and Dorothy to record it together. This turned out to be a shrewd move because it entered the charts in 1961.

The song had been penned with her pianist Ernie Dunstal, although, I don't think Ernie ever got a penny in royalties. She'd bunged him fifty quid for his input. Years later when she was feeling a bit maudlin, she told him that she was sorry for cutting him out of the copyright and promised she would contact the publishers the next day to put things right. Dot would promise you the world when she was in a good mood but the next day completely forget about it and that's just what she did; she completely forgot about it. When Ernie went to the publishers to sign the contract he found that she hadn't signed anything over to him at all.

Dorothy continued to promote 'Say It With Flowers', doing the rounds of radio stations and appearing on TV. Contact between Roger and Dot became less and less frequent; Dorothy wasn't sure where he was. Hilda, her secretary, sarcastically quipped, 'Ring the best hotel in Yugoslavia, he's sure to be there.' Determined to find out where he was Dorothy decided to go to Roger's father's apartment off Shooter's Hill in Bexleyheath. On arriving at the apartment block, she bumped into one of the residents. The woman, recognising Dorothy, told her that if she was looking for Mr Moore, he'd been taken to the Woolwich War Memorial Hospital. Dorothy said that she didn't know that her father-in-law was ill. The woman informed her that it wasn't George, Roger's father, who was ill but Roger. Dorothy was stunned by this information; unbeknown to her, Roger had been back in the country for some time. He'd been taken ill on location and been flown home with kidney problems. Dorothy was as mad as hell. She stormed into the hospital and confronted him: 'Why the hell didn't you let me know you were ill? Christ! I didn't even know you were back in the fucking country? When did you get back from Zagreb? Have you been seeing someone in Yugoslavia?' Ever the joker, Roger quipped, 'Sure, Marshal Tito.'

In truth he'd been seeing an actress on the set called Luisa Mattioli and they'd fallen in love. The way that Dorothy found out would have made a good plot for a film. After Roger had been discharged, a bunch of letters addressed to him had been forwarded to Bexley from the hospital. They had Italian postmarks so Dorothy, suspecting the worst, opened them. She couldn't understand a word but the kisses on the bottom told her she was in trouble. She recalled:

I'd just come from the Talk of the Town; it was the top cabaret venue in London. Rene, my sister was downstairs with Ernie, my pianist; Rene was cooking supper after the show – bacon and eggs and whatever. I went upstairs to get out of my clothes and have a quick shower.

When I came down I noticed an envelope, which had been forwarded from the Woolwich War Memorial Hospital. So I opened the envelope and there were four other letters inside tied together but they'd been posted on separate days – consecutive days and they were addressed to Roger Moore Film Star in very small writing and of course it had the Italian stamp on it. When I read what I did read it knocked me for six. They were all in Italian but I could understand bits of it; musical terms are written in Italian; Tutti means *all over* and I could imagine the rest. I called the maître d' at the Astor Club who was a mate of mine.

I would go into the Astor Club whenever I had a week out. I would only have to call Bertie Green the owner and he would put me on. Anyway, I called the maître d', I knew he was Italian and I asked him to translate the letters for me. He said he would but when he read them he said, 'You don't want to know what's in these Dot; they're pretty grim'. I said I want to know. Well when I heard what *was* in them I wish I hadn't asked. She was saying where she had kissed him all over and what she hadn't done to him … well you can guess. She [Luisa] said if 'Doritty doesn't believe that we are in love show her these letters'. And I thought what kind of a woman would do that. I was devastated they [the letters] confirmed my worst fears; this wasn't just one of his dalliances, this time Roger had fallen in love.

When I found all this out Roger was still filming *The Saint*. My father had just died and it hurt me a great deal that Roger didn't come to his funeral, nor did his mother and father; it hurt me a great deal because his mother and father loved Bexley; they were down every weekend – Friday, Saturday, Sunday and go back Monday. Anyway it hurt me a hell of a lot … My father's last words to me were, 'Roger has been to see me on his big white horse,' and the next day when I went in he was dead … My father adored him. It was a very traumatic time for me; and all this, not long after the split; on top of which I was running out of money; all the money I earned in America was put into a joint account and I had no money of my own … I hadn't worked much in England. I decided the only thing to do was to give Roger a divorce; if I could get a settlement at least I'd have some money to start again.

So, I went out to the studios in my Ford Thunderbird that I'd brought back from America. I was in a beautiful lemon suit and I was slim, not through diet, may I say but through my situation. I saw the commissionaire and I said 'I'm Mrs Moore' and he said he would get someone to take me on set. I didn't know it at the time but she [Luisa] was there. So Roger came out and I asked him if we could get a cup of tea or something.

He got me a cup of tea out of the machine in one of those paper cup things. I said you can have a divorce, Roger, for £5,000; I need the money; I haven't got any, not to speak of anyway and I want to start again. He said he didn't have it; 'I can't afford it,' he said and went back on set … I got in my car and drove a little way. I was so upset I was shaking so I pulled into a lay-by. Then I saw his car pass and turn right. Luisa was with him. I put my head on the steering wheel and broke my heart. I wasn't one to cry in public, it was either get up or die. I felt like dying at the time with my brother gone and my father gone but I wasn't a person to cry in public and although I felt like dying at the time, it inspired me to write this song:

> Where can I go, and find me a place
> For wherever I go, I still see your face
> I must go on, find a place in the sun
> As time is my friend, till this battle is won

Dorothy, ever the professional continued to fulfil her contract at the Talk of the Town. She was just due to go on stage when Roger appeared in her dressing room and dropped a bombshell; he told her that there was no easy way to say it, but he was moving in with Luisa. He offered her a cheque saying that it might pay a few bills. Dorothy completely lost it, 'I don't need your fucking money,' she screamed and ripped the cheque up into little pieces and flung it back in his face. Then, tearing her wedding ring from her fingers, she yelled, 'And you can take this as well you fucking whoremaster,' and hurled it after the retreating figure of her unfaithful husband.

Like all performers Dorothy knew that the show had to go on. So, with tears streaming down her face, she made her entrance. The Talk of the Town in those days was arranged in a cabaret style with the audience sat at tables eating dinner. Dorothy was half way through her act when a drunk sat at one of the tables yelled 'Not another one'. In no mood to be heckled by a Hooray Henry trying to impress his underdressed, overdeveloped, much younger girlfriend, Dot coolly walked from the stage, threaded her way through the audience towards the heckler, cupped her hands over his ear and whispered something. The audience, knowing Dorothy's reputation for the acerbic putdown, started to titter. The man, realising he was the source of their merriment, looked suitably embarrassed and clammed up. With a look of satisfaction on her face, Dorothy returned to the stage, walked back to the microphone and prepared to sing her next song. Ernie, her pianist, asked her what she'd said to him. 'I called him a cunt,' she whispered with a sassy smile. All the musicians wanted to know what she'd said and the word went through the fifteen-piece band like a Mexican wave. When it reached the drummer he quipped, 'Which cunt does she mean?' Dorothy broke up laughing, her troubles forgotten … for a while at any rate.

Sometime later Roger turned up at Bexley to get some of his things. Dorothy's secretary, Hilda remembers:

I was with Dorothy by the swimming pool when Roger arrived. Dorothy stormed up stairs leaving Roger and I stood just under the bedroom window. She stuffed a load of his clothes into a suitcase and hurled it out of the window yelling, 'Fuck off you whoremaster and don't come back.' The case hit Roger in the back of the neck. I wanted to laugh but it was no laughing matter.

When Roger went Dorothy was inconsolable. Trying to calm her down, I told her that he would be back. 'No,' she said, 'he won't and it's all my fault for not going with him to Zagreb.'

Dorothy thought by calling his bluff he would come back. 'And when he does,' she said, 'I'll slam the door right in his fucking face.' She didn't mean a word of it; she would have taken him back with open arms. She often said that she'd given him to the 'Italian Dame' on a plate. Dorothy said:

> I must have been fucking mad. I should have fought for him; it was like giving a kid sweets then hitting him over the head for eating them. After all I had the advantage, I knew Roger, I'd lived with him for nine years. The one thing I should never have done was to pack his bags and tell him to fuck off.

Dorothy was so obsessed with getting Roger back that when she found out from her dressmaker, Douggie Darnell, that he'd set up home with Luisa in a house in Mill Hill she decided to confront him. Determined to look her best when she faced the beautiful Luisa, Dorothy entered her walk-in wardrobe and sifted through her clothes one by one. Then, finding what she was looking for, an elegant dress, she threw it on the bed and chose a pair of shoes to match. She was determined to show Roger what he was missing. She started to dress slowly, meticulously. Finally she went to the dressing table and applied her makeup. Then, rummaging in her jewellery box, she pulled out a fine gold ankle chain with two entwined hearts upon it; the inscription read 'From Roger with Love'. She clasped it around her ankle then finished her preparation by spraying herself with Joy perfume. She looked in the mirror and then satisfied with the result yelled, 'Come on Hilda let's get this fucking show on the road,' and set off in her powder blue Ford Thunderbird. When Dorothy and Hilda arrived, Roger wouldn't answer the door. Dorothy proceeded to hurl stones, smashing every window in the house. Roger came down to try to restrain her but she grabbed him by the throat; 'Your hand is bleeding,' he croaked. Dorothy full of Welsh drama cried, 'It's my heart that's bleeding.' She told me that as she was picking the glass out of her skin in the bath, the water ran red with her blood – she always was very dramatic.

When trying to smash her way into Roger and Luisa's life didn't work she took the desperate decision to take Roger to court for restoration of conjugal rights. She'd found the ancient precedent in an old law book. There was no way the law could be enforced but Dot was determined to follow it through. Amazingly Dorothy won the case and Roger was ordered to hop back into her bed. It was an unenforceable order of course in which Roger had no intention of complying, but it was the start of Dorothy's obsessive quest to get him back and she vowed that she would never ever grant him a divorce. She would never admit it but she never really got over losing him. The few affairs she had after Roger left didn't really mean anything. I'm sure had the shoe been on the other foot and Dorothy had left Roger, things would have been very different. Like most big stars Dorothy had total tunnel vision where her career was concerned; when she was on the road that was all that mattered. She could be away for weeks on end and rarely ring home to see how Roger was, but now he'd gone it was a very different matter. It wasn't just the fact that he'd left her for a younger woman, she felt betrayed; she'd put her life and career on hold to promote his and now at the age of nearly 50 she had to pull herself up by the bootstraps and start again.

After Roger's exit Dorothy fell into a deep depression. She felt she had nothing to live for; she wouldn't get out of bed for months. Her doctor prescribed her an antidepressant drug called Dexamyl, a mixture of amphetamine and barbiturates. They were legal in the sixties but little did the doctor or Dorothy know that it would lead to her being hooked on the drug for the rest of her life. The drugs were the uppers of choice in those days, much like Es are today. They were nicknamed Purple Hearts by the Mod subculture on account that they looked like a heart and were purple in colour. Purple Hearts were used extensively by the showbiz fraternity, especially by pop groups who, because of demanding tours, would have to drive all night to get to their gigs. The drug often led to bouts of psychosis and they were banned in 1973. After the ban, Dorothy's dependency on them drove her to buy them on the black market. She had a bent chemist in her pocket and would often come home with a bunch of them wrapped up in a tissue declaring that she had just got some more of her dolly mixtures.

The happy pills worked for a while but they couldn't hide the fact that she was still desperately unhappy. The grief-stricken Dorothy, not caring if she lived or died, decided to throw herself into charity work and when she was asked by her old friend, Billy Smart, if she would sing in a cage with six live tigers to raise money for the Variety Club, her response was: 'Why not, what have I got to lose – now that the prick has left me, I don't care if the fucking tigers claw me.'

The audience that night read like a who's who of British show business: Bruce Forsyth, film stars Dennis Price and Stanley Baker, the magician David Nixon, Sir Billy Butlin, The Beverley Sisters, Hattie Jakes, Erick Sykes and Jon Pertwee. Roger was there too. When Bruce Forsyth joked that he hoped Roger had taken out insurance, Roger, responding with his usual acerbic wit quipped, 'Yes on the six tigers.'

In 1963 Dorothy decided to use St Mary's Mount as a venue for a spectacular charity show called *Fiesta 63*. It was in aid of Dr Clark's Memorial Fund, which was researching into kidney transplantation. Dorothy's only brother, Fred, whom she loved dearly, was stuck down with nephritis and on 22 December 1955 he died, at the relatively young age of 37.

Dorothy blamed Fred's kidney complaint on the fact that he'd caught malaria while serving in Burma. He had enlisted in the Blues and Royals at 18 and was posted to Burma during the war. Dorothy did her bit for the war effort too, singing for the troops. She sang at Biggin Hill just before the famous Thousand-bomber Raid and told me:

It was sad to see so many young boys not yet men, dressed in their uniforms, with their kit on their lap, just waiting for their names to be called. As a number came up on a screen, someone would leave the theatre and I wondered how many of them would come back to their families. In the bar, where personal tankards of the airmen hung, some were turned over as a heart-rending reminder of the ones that didn't make it and it occurred to me as I sang to these brave boys, that I may never see my only brother again.

Dorothy missed Fred terribly and was determined to raise money in his name, she recalled:

> My brother was six foot three; you would have taken a lease on his life. There were no kidney transplants in those days and he wouldn't come with me to the doctor. I was over from America at this point and he came to lunch. I could see how ill he was and asked him to come to the doctors with me. He agreed and the doctor said 'you haven't brought him to me too soon.' I knew he was ill but I didn't know he was on the danger list … He died at Christmas time.

Dorothy didn't go to the funeral, she didn't go to her mother's either; she couldn't face funerals, or perhaps it was her own mortality she couldn't face. The only one she went to was her father's and that was only because she thought Roger would be there. To her chagrin he never showed. Dorothy was very upset and told her sister Rene: 'Dada thought the world of Roger. I thought he would turn up. Perhaps the man upstairs will forgive him but I fuckin' won't, not ever.'

Determined to raise as much as she could for the cause, she contacted all her showbiz friends. The place was awash with the stars of the day – Frank Ifield, Cliff Richard, Russ Conway, Diana Dors all the cast of *Z Cars*; the list was endless. Most of the people stayed the night. There were twenty-two men sleeping upstairs and about the same number of women sleeping downstairs. Stalls were set up around the swimming pool: coconut shies, hoopla stalls and hot dog stands, the scene was reminiscent of the fairgrounds she knew as a girl. On the steps of the patio, which looked on to the pool, she'd set up a stage for the concert that was to follow. The tickets sold like hot cakes, bought by the locals who were eager to meet all the stars. Dorothy contacted Leslie Grade, who was one of the directors of ATV at the time, to ask him to televise the event but she was told that it was too short notice to change the schedules. You can imagine how mad she was when she found out that on the night in question ATV had screened an old film. When, some years later, Leslie Grade had a heart attack she sent him a telegram saying: 'Impossible you haven't got a heart.' Only Dot would have had the nerve to insult one of the biggest agents in Britain and get away with it.

Dorothy's efforts to keep herself occupied couldn't mask the fact that she was still desperately unhappy. She continued to self medicate on her 'dolly mixtures'. *My* first experience of Purple Hearts came years later when I was going through a rather acrimonious divorce. I had just come back from Australia and went straight from Heathrow Airport to Dorothy's house. Everybody went to Auntie Dot if they were in trouble; she always had a sympathetic ear for any of her friends in trouble and I was no exception. I remember it like it was yesterday; we were sitting drinking tea in her kitchen at Bray. I told her my woes and she gave her usual response, 'Put a new song in your act.' I said, 'Will it cure me?' 'No,' she said with a chuckle, 'but it might take your mind off it.' I'd arrived on the day she was about to record an album at Abbey Road for Norman Newell and she insisted I go with her, saying that I shouldn't be alone in the state I was in. She said it would be good for me to listen to nice music and forget my troubles for a while. It was the worst thing I could have done; listening to Dorothy wringing every emotion out of her torch songs had me crying like a baby. The songs she recorded reflected the way she was feeling after Roger left. Especially poignant was her rendition of 'Is That All There Is'. Dorothy recalled:

When I sang 'Is That All There Is' it was the hardest thing I had ever done. There wasn't much time left; Norman said we only had about fifteen minutes left of studio time before the guys [musicians] would run into overtime. I told him I couldn't do it in the time; I wouldn't be able to do it justice. I dreaded it because it was all out of rhythm and I had to count the bars so as not to miss a beat. I'd rehearsed the song so much; I'd marked on my score where my breath had to come and so on. I did the first take and I wasn't satisfied; I wanted to do another one because the emotion had got to me and I'd started to cry when it got to the part about the fire. When I finished Norman asked me to go into the box to listen; I said Norman, I'll do it better tomorrow. So I didn't listen to it that night; it had been a long session and I wanted to get home. When we went in the next day Norman played me the first take; it was so emotional that we kept it and it became the master for the record.

It was a great session; Norman had got the best out of Dorothy that day and the album, *Rain Rain Go Away*, took the award that year for best female middle-of-the-road album. As I was driving Dot home after the recording session it started to snow. Dorothy, noticing a look of despair on my face, asked me what was wrong. I spilled my guts about how my life was in ruins. She said she understood perfectly: 'Think what Roger did to me,' she croaked. With that she ordered me to stop the car. 'I can't stop on the M4 motorway,' I protested but she was adamant. So I pulled onto the hard shoulder, Dorothy jumped out, grabbed a handful of snow, rammed a Purple Heart into my mouth followed by the snow, then took one herself and we continued towards Bray as high as kites, my ex-wife and Roger forgotten for the time being.

The next time she would cross swords with Roger was in court, over some love letters that he'd sent her during their marriage. Dorothy was intending to include them in her autobiography, which was never published. Roger took out an injunction against her, successfully preventing her from including them in her book. Although Dorothy owned the letters the court ruled that because Roger had written them they were his copyright, and Moore versus Squires has become the precedent for that particular law to this day. She also tried to include the love letters from Luisa to Roger, which had been forwarded to St Mary's Mount but an injunction served on her by Luisa was upheld and she wasn't allowed to include those in her ill-fated book either.

After the verdict Dorothy, crying as usual, said she couldn't understand why Roger would want the letters excluded from the book. 'They are beautiful letters,' she sobbed, 'love letters from a husband to a wife, written during a wonderful marriage. If it was ever doubted that he loved me, and only married me to become a star, then these letters prove otherwise.' Knowing she couldn't win this particular case, she announced plans to sue Roger for £3 million in the American courts for loss of royalties. 'The publication of my book has been held up by Roger's action,' she said, 'I've had to turn down work to the tune of £75,000 during the five months that this hearing has been going on.' She didn't win this case either but the vendetta continued. Dorothy would sue at the least provocation. Alone in her library, watching the 1969 BAFTAs on television, she was incensed when she saw Kenneth More introducing Roger and Luisa Mattioli as Mr and Mrs Moore. They had been living together for some years as man and wife and she'd borne him two children but they weren't legally married. Dorothy had granted Roger a divorce in 1968, but she was still legally entitled to call herself Mrs Moore so she decided to sue Kenneth More in the High Court for libel.

Kenneth knew that Roger had been married to Dorothy, but so far as the world was concerned, Roger and Luisa were man and wife. It's debatable if Kenneth More knew that Roger and Luisa weren't married but when asked about the case later he quipped, 'What could I say, here's Roger Moore and his mistress?' A few weeks later Kenneth received a letter from Dorothy's solicitors claiming that he had slandered their client by introducing Roger and Luisa as man and wife on national television. Kenneth wrote a letter of apology to Dorothy but this didn't appease her, she decided to sue him in the High Court anyway. Her defence was as bizarre as the case was trivial. Colin Duncan, Dorothy's QC, told the court:

> The words in the television program i.e. *The British Academy Awards Cinema Special* on Granada TV, implied that Miss Squires was not married to Mr Moore and was therefore tantamount to saying that she (Dorothy) had been deceitful in holding herself out to be his wife and had been living in immoral co-habitation.

Kenneth More, defended by his wartime navel friend, Michael Havers QC, denied the libel saying that: 'The words used in the programme were not defamatory.' Mr Duncan QC continued: 'Miss Squires has known Mr Kenneth More for a long time and he knew that she was married to Roger Moore and I submit that you publish an apology and pay Miss Squires cost and a sum of compensation.'

Kenneth More agreed to the apology and costs and the case continued. Ironically on the same day Roger was at Caxton Hall marrying for the third time, this time to Luisa Mattioli. The case continued in October of that year. The jury took just 30 minutes to decide that Kenneth More had not been defamatory and the case was dismissed, resulting in Dorothy having to pay £3,000 in costs. Dorothy spent much of her fortune on legal fees. She undertook thirty court cases over fifteen years, the most trivial being against Roger for the aforementioned restoration of conjugal rights case.

6

Other Suitors

After Roger left there had been a few dalliances; a handful of hopefuls trying to fill his shoes – two of whom were Mark Eden and Simon Oates, both actors in the Roger mould. Dorothy met Mark in 1963 at a mutual friend's house and invited him to one of her parties and they ended up in bed together. The affair was doomed from the start. Like Roger he was much younger than Dot, eighteen years to be precise. I don't think she was Mark's type either, in his words: 'She was loud and brash and swore like a trooper.' She countered by saying she couldn't stand the way he burped all the time but there must have been some chemistry between them and they began a stormy affair, which was often punctuated with violent arguments, reminiscent of the Dot and Roger years.

It was like history repeating itself in more ways than one; she was on the rebound from Roger when she met Mark, much as she'd been on the rebound from Billy when she met Roger. For all her apparent self-confidence, it seems she was very immature when it came to men. She would become infatuated like a teenager and possessive to the point of obsession. When Dorothy found out that Mark had become a bit too friendly with an actress he was working with, she went ballistic. When the affair was over Dorothy didn't want to believe it. Dorothy tried everything to get Mark back. She bombarded him with pleading phone calls for weeks. When this didn't work she got me to drive her to Mark's mother's house in Ramsgate where she lavished gifts on his son, David. She would do anything to ingratiate herself to Mark; she even took David onstage with her at the Palladium to sing 'My Best Boy', from *Auntie Mame*, and would often invite him to stay at St Mary's Mount to swim in the pool. I don't know if Mark ever knew it but I had to fish him out of the water once because he was at risk of drowning.

After a while the phone calls stopped, but if Mark thought that she'd mellowed he was in for a rude awakening. After a successful recording session Dorothy, on a high, decided to ring Mark to ask him to join her for a drink – for old time's sake she said. Against his better judgment, he agreed and after a couple of glasses of champagne Dot offered to drive him home. Once he was in the car she locked the doors, effectively taking him hostage and tore off at break-neck speed. After a hair-raising ride through the streets of London and out into the Kent countryside, she suddenly screeched to a shuddering halt, opened the door and told him to get out, or words to that effect. She left him stranded in the middle of nowhere. Dot once told me that revenge was sweet and she had certainly got her own back on the unsuspecting Mark.

Dorothy and Mark may not have been suited romantically but they were artistically and with Ernie Dunstall, her musical director, they wrote a musical together called *Old Rowley* which was based on the life of Charles II. Dorothy had this romantic Barbara Cartland vision of history, especially where Charles II was concerned and her ambition was to get the musical produced by 1966, which would have been the anniversary of the Great Fire of London. Once Dorothy had an idea she would tenaciously pursue it with every contact she had. Dot approached Dorothy and Phil Solomon, the agents for the Bachelors and Lena Zavaroni. They were hardnosed agents who'd seen it all but when Dorothy sang them the songs from the score they had tears in their eyes. Dorothy could really sell a song and she sold the idea of *Old Rowley* to Phil and Dorothy Solomon, for an advance of £3,000. The money was spent on making an album of the score with her singing all the solos, Mark narrating the story, Ernie accompanying on piano and the Mike Sam Singers doing the choral work. It was a wonderful score but for all Dots' efforts it was never produced. I don't know what ever happened to it; perhaps it will surface one day and she'll have a posthumous hit show to add to her long list of credits.

The following foreword for *Old Rowley* was written by Dot. I hope you will forgive me for subjecting you to this diatribe but Dorothy had discovered *Rogét's Thesaurus* – if you'll excuse the pun – and thought, wrongly, that to be noticed she had to elbow in every long and complicated word that would fit. This stemmed from a deep inferiority complex about her education. Dorothy had left school at 15 and thought she had to prove herself. In my opinion, she had a very high IQ and could have succeeded with anything she put her mind to. Anyway here is the foreword to *Old Rowley*:

I shall always be morally indebted to the enterprising entrepreneur Philip Solomon for his blind faith and belief that Mark Eden, Ernie Dunstall and I were capable of composing and writing the score of the musical. When he told us the leading man of Mark was to be his favourite monarch Charles II, I couldn't wait to get started, for his majesty Charles II had always been my blue-eyed boy, especially when he helped me to reach number one in the school history charts.

Philip Solomon and his wife have guided and managed many successful stars and in their stable of two legged runners are three very successful men bearing the yeomanly title 'The Bachelors'. At the time Mr Solomon approached us in 1965, Mark Ernie and I had collaborated in the writing of songs two of which were recorded by the Bachelors so, having mutually agreed to attempt this giant assignment, I volunteered to burn the midnight oil and became the autoptical dedicated bloodhound, committing myself to the herculean task of the perquisition into the life of this great monarch. On reflection I smile when I think of the time Philip Solomon mailed me a short play, in book form and written by that talented genius the wry Bernard Shaw. The play dealt with the latter few years of Charles' life. Written on the enclosed compliments slip were the words 'get cracking'.

Whenever the mercurial, impatient Philip Solomon played stork to a creative idea, it had to be delivered in a matter of days with complete disregard to the constructive incubating period and further reflection, not having been involved in the creation of a musical before, we, the brewing architects of the score, started in the cart before the horse methodology; completely oblivious to the problems we were creating for the potential author of the stage play.

I have seen many plays and movies depicting the life of Charles II, he was always portrayed as a profligate. Even his devoted subjects dubbed him with the jocular nickname of 'Old Rowley'. Rowley was his beloved stallion who covered the mares in the Royal stables. Charles II was profoundly fond of racing and Rowley never failed to be the first past the winning post. So, like his royal owner, he too went down in history. The famous Rowley mile at Newmarket racecourse is named after the illustrious Rowley. In over 300 years there's never been a monarch crowned his majesty Charles III and synonymously in over three hundred years there's never been a stallion carrying his owner's colours called Rowley.

We the British are fortunate to have in our midst the future Charles III and I am the fortunate owner of a beautiful young stallion whose name will appear on the race cards as Old Rowley and is a lucky fellow to have as his trainer the very dedicated Miss Jenny Pitman.

Having intruded on the privacy of his majesty Charles II, my posthumous love for him knows no bounds and I somehow feel I've qualified to enter into an occasional royal 'Pow-wow' with his majesty regarding my youngster [her horse] and as I am a believer in divination I don't have to tell him I took on a great responsibility when I named my horse Old Rowley. During my pleasurable endless hours of research it came through loud and clear that Charles II was a very popular admired monarch. He indulgently had the happiness and prosperity of his subjects close to his heart and his lot was indeed a sad lot for a king. Hopefully my stage play will depict the many reasons for Charles' sexual pranks. His mistresses were many, the most reputable being the congenial Nell Gwynne; Nell was the only royal concubine, Charles' Queen, Catherine of Braganza, accepted and in fact she became very fond of the witty lady. Nell, unlike her contemporaries, was never avaricious and asked for nothing from her King. Charles' time honoured phrase, which he whispered on his deathbed, 'Let not poor Nell starve', is the burden of proof.

After the brief affair with Mark Eden, next on the list was Keith Miller. The first time she met Keith he was the pianist with the Hedley Ward Trio. They were an act in their own right but on this occasion they were the house band at Paul Raymond's Celebrity restaurant in Conduit Street in the West End of London. I was doing a week's cabaret there with Dakota Staten, the American Jazz singer, and staying, as usual, with Dorothy. At the time Dorothy was trying to get me a record deal so she decided to come to the show, bringing with her Norman Newel, her record producer. She sat in the front row and laughed and applauded everything I did, especially when I did an impersonation of her. When Dakota came on it was a different story; she stared at her in a most intimidating manner then turned her attention to Keith on the piano. Dorothy was a sucker for anyone with talent and Keith was a fantastic pianist; he was like an orchestra on his own.

I introduced them after the show and not long after that meeting Keith became Dorothy's musical boyfriend. Contrary to popular opinion though, Dot wasn't promiscuous. People thought, because of her habitual swearing, she was an easy lay. Nothing could have been further from the truth. Dorothy was a real paradox when it came to morals; she would tell someone to fuck off without hesitation but couldn't bring herself to use the word as a verb, as the Anglo-Saxons had intended it. Keith Miller had taken over from Ernie Dunstall as her musical director, when he left to play for Vince Hill at the Talk of The Town. Ernie had promised to play for Dot at a club in Islington that week and had completely forgotten about it. Dot was furious; she'd known Ernie since he was a teenager and thought this to be another betrayal. To be fair to Ernie, Dot wasn't working regularly enough to keep him in full-time employment and when Vince offered him the job he had no option but to take it. Dorothy, in a fit of pique, rang Ernie's father, Arnold, and threatened to blacken Ernie's name. 'He'll never work again,' she screamed. Ernie's father, incensed by this attack on his son, told her in no mean terms that if he had to work for the rest of his life to support his son he would do it rather than have him beholden to a fucking old has-been like her. This broke Dot's heart. She loved Ernie, not in the biblical sense I hasten to add. He'd been with her, through good times and bad and now, when she felt she needed him most, he'd gone.

After Vince Hill, Ernie went on to become the musical director for singer and impersonator Joe Longthorne. When Joe sang 'Say It With Flowers' on his TV show in 1991, he innocently announced that it had been written by his musical director Ernie Dunstal. Dorothy was furious. She knew Ernie had a hand in writing the song, nevertheless, she tried to sue both Joe and Central Independent Television saying, unfathomably, that Joe was part of a conspiracy and that his statement was and I quote: 'A malicious act of contempt of court likely to prejudice a fair trial and, as conspiracy is quite evident, there is a common law offence of attempting to defeat the course of justice.' Dorothy had bought a book of Court Practice Volume 1 and 2 and the volumes of a book containing County Court Practice. Consequently she thought she knew everything about the law but as the saying goes 'a little knowledge is a dangerous thing'. Dorothy was always a bit paranoid but this attack on Joe Longthorne proved that it had really begun to manifest itself, which is borne out by the letter she sent to Leslie Hill, the managing director of Central Television. I won't subject you to the whole seven-page epistle – even I, who have known her all my life and understood how her mind worked, cannot entirely fathom out the connection. She mixed the cases against Rupert Murdoch, her bankruptcy, the Joe Longthorne case, her eviction from her home in Bray, her concert in Brighton and goodness knows what else in an effort to make a case against Joe. I'm sure the executives at Central Television wouldn't have been able to make head nor tail of it. However, she did receive an apology from Tony Wolf, the controller of Central.

She had other MDs, all great musicians: Will Fyffe Jnr, Kenny Brown, Bert Waller and Keith Miller but no one could replace her 'lovely Ernie'. Dorothy had taken him under her wing when he was just a kid and taught him the business. But true to form Dorothy never bore a grudge for long and she and Ernie stayed friends for the rest of her life. He never MD'd for her again but he was always there for her when she needed him and it was Ernie she called upon when she wanted some special material written for her famous comeback concert at the London Palladium. Undoubtedly one of the hits of that show was the *Irony of War*, a 15-minute medley of war songs that had been routined by Ernie and arranged by Nicky Welch. It brought the house down. Dorothy had written the lighting plot for it. She'd learnt a lot during her long career in the theatre and any lighting plot that she'd seen, would be written down for future use. This knowledge was never more evident than when she did the *Irony of War*. It was a complicated routine with quite a few changes in key and tempo and it took Dot about two weeks to write the plot. The combined talents of Ernie's routine, Nicky's arrangement and Dorothy's lighting culminated in 15 minutes of magnificent theatre that received the much deserved standing ovation it got.

Keith Miller had introduced Dorothy to Nicky Welch, a wonderful musician and arranger who became her musical director for the rest of her recording career. Previously he'd been part of a four-part harmony group called the Frazer Hayes Four. He'd also worked as a comedy double act called Don and Nichols. I'd worked with them on the Butlin's circuit in the early sixties; little did I know that the next time I would work with Nicky he would be the musical director at the London Palladium. Keith was due to be her accompanist that night until things went wrong and the relationship broke up. Dorothy had not only lost her lover in Keith but now she was without a pianist as well. Keith was a great guy but he was a habitual womaniser. I'm not suggesting he didn't have feelings for Dot but to him it was just a bit of fun. To Dorothy, however, it was more serious. Keith was much younger than Dot; it was obvious by now that she had a predilection for younger guys and the relationship soon started showing cracks. Dorothy, knowing that her relationship was on borrowed time, was trying every trick in the book to please him, she would even send herself flowers and pretend they were from an admirer, just to make him jealous. One night, when the atmosphere was particularly cool, she offered to make him steak au poivre for dinner but she'd forgotten that she'd offered me the steak the day before and I'd eaten it. 'I've eaten the steak,' I said. She went bloody ballistic and called me a greedy bastard. 'But you told me to eat it,' I protested. 'I didn't want you to eat the fuckin' lot,' she screamed.

In retrospect I think the reason for her outburst wasn't because I'd eaten the steak but because of the situation between her and Keith and the only one around to lash out at was me. She was always sorry afterwards and when I walked out, slapping a fiver on the table, telling her to buy some more fucking steak, Dorothy spent the next two months trying to find me. She'd ring up London Management, my agent at the time, and badger them to tell her where I was. When they wouldn't divulge my whereabouts she'd ring all my friends. She finally found me when she went to President Records in Denmark Street, who we both recorded for, and as if nothing had happened said, 'Are you coming home tonight?' Dot could have a row with you and ten minutes later offer to make you a cup of tea as if nothing had happened. When we got back to St Mary's Mount Keith was there but the atmosphere was cool. I'm sure Dot only asked me to come home with her for moral support; there was always an ulterior motive with Dot.

The break-up finally came on New Year's Eve. It was very late, all the guests had gone and I had gone to bed. I was awoken by Dorothy screaming fit to burst a blood vessel. She had a great pair of lungs on her – she wasn't known in show business as the 'Iron Lung' for nothing. To indicate how loud she was screaming; I was in bed on the other side of the twenty-two-room house and she was in the drive. I rushed down stairs in time to see Keith in his car with the engine running. Dorothy was standing in front of it yelling: 'You can't fucking leave me on New Year's Eve, you'll have to run over me first.' Keith accelerated, Dot jumped out of the way and Keith was off up the road.

Dorothy ran sobbing into the kitchen and frantically started scattering the contents of the cupboards in search of pills screaming: 'I'm going to knock myself off.' Before I could stop her she'd opened a bottle of codeine and swallowed half the contents. I grabbed the pills from her. She ran upstairs and collapsed onto the bed and fell into a coma-like sleep. I was frightened to death. I didn't know what to do; should I ring 999? If I rang and she was OK she would play hell so I just lay by her side on the bed listening to her heavy breathing. After a while her breathing became more regular but I slept by her side all night just in case. In the morning she woke up as right as rain and said: 'Hi John what do you want for breakfast?'

St Mary's Mount had become a much more sombre place since Keith had gone, not least because Dot had fallen into a deep depression again. She went days without speaking; she just slopped about the house all day in her dressing gown. I know she must have missed Keith, I missed him too; I missed his jokes, our impromptu sessions when we would gather around the white grand piano and sing out with gusto. I missed him not being there when I came home from the theatre – he would make Dot stay up until I came home because he said it wasn't right for me to come back after work to a dark house. But he'd gone and try as I might I couldn't lift Dot's melancholy mood. She wouldn't leave the house. In retrospect I think she was probably bipolar; when she was on a high she was the life and soul of the party but at other times she was, to use a musical term, very tacet.

Dorothy's mood finally lifted; my numerous attempts to get her to go out had paid off. She capitulated and asked me to take her to the Players Restaurant, a haunt of actors, in the West End. She'd had a tip off that Roger might be there but when he didn't show, her mood deepened again and she took it out on the waiter. He suggested we try the duck. 'I hope it's better than the last fucking duck I had here,' she snapped. During the meal she made one holy mess of the tablecloth, tearing the duck with her bare hands and ripping the bread to bits; there were crumbs and bits of duck everywhere. When the waiter courteously asked if she would like him to change the cloth she told him to fuck off. Then, assuming that I had finished, grabbed the remains of my duck and started to attack the morsels of meat still left on its carcass. Throwing some notes on the table she said, 'Let's go to Danny's Club, I haven't seen him in ages.' So off we went in search of Danny La Rue's nightclub in the West End.

I was navigating her large silver-grey Chrysler Barracuda around the narrow streets of Soho when I realised we were lost. Seeing a tout on the door of a strip club, I asked him if he knew where the Two Deck Club was. He said he had no idea and why didn't we go to his club instead. 'You must be fucking kidding,' Dorothy yelled, 'can't you find anything better to do than sell tits for a living!' We drove on until, on seeing a hooker, Dot insisted I ask *her*. 'Do you know where the Two Deck Club is?' I asked. 'I no speak a da' fuckin English you twat,' was her terse reply. Dot broke up laughing; it was the first time I'd seen her smile since Keith had left. When we eventually arrived at Danny's Club, Jack, Danny's partner and manager, greeted us. Dot introduced me as her nephew. 'What did you do that for?' I asked. 'Well, you know what people are like; they'll think I've pulled another young bloke.' Dot could be very insecure at times.

7

The Comeback

It had been a long, hard climb back to the top for Dorothy. She'd been out of the public eye for almost ten years, seven of which had been in Hollywood with Roger. On returning to Britain she found that she had been mostly forgotten by the public and the money was running out fast. The cost of running St Mary's Mount alone was enormous. Gigs were few and far between. Rock 'n' roll was at its height and there wasn't much call for torch singers like Dorothy. But she was resourceful; whenever she was short of money she would sell one of her songs. Dot was one hell of a saleswoman and could waltz into any publisher in London, demand an advance for one of her songs and invariably walk out £100 the richer. It was soon spent though but when anyone criticised Dorothy for being extravagant she would quip, 'It's only a line in a song'. Dot wrote upwards of 130 songs. The American songwriter, Rod McKuen, really rated Dorothy and he wrote on his website:

Dorothy was indeed fabulous, in every sense of the word. On stage she gave every song she sang a new perspective. And what a voice! There must be something in the Welsh to have produced Dorothy, Shirley Bassey and

Tom Jones, to name but a few of the great vocalists that hail from South Wales. I loved her version of 'Solitude's My Home', a song I wrote, no one has ever performed it better. A producer and I wanted to record Dorothy but we never got around to it.

Dorothy was nothing if not tenacious; in her own words she was 'always up at the count of nine.' And so, armed with songs she'd written with Ernie Dunstall, she decided to try her luck in America and set sail on the *Queen Mary* for New York. She and Ernie arrived at the Brill Building armed with a bunch of manuscripts and went about plugging their songs to hardnosed publishers. The Brill Building was located at 1619 Broadway on 49th Street in the theatre district of New York City, just north of Times Square. The area was known as Tin Pan Alley, much like Denmark Street was in London. Unlike Denmark Street, where Dorothy was well known, this was unknown territory and they soon found out it was going to be a different ball game. The building was the centre of activity for the popular music industry, especially music publishing and song writing, and the home of such luminaries as Leiber and Stoller, Carole King and Neil Sedaka. Unfortunately, Dorothy's foray into the American music industry wasn't very successful; I think it cost her more to promote her songs than she made by selling them. One that she did sell was to Gene Goodman, brother of Benny Goodman, the famous band leader. He'd been a friend of Dorothy's since her time in Hollywood with Roger and was the publisher of her theme for the film *Tammy Tell Me True*. Alas the song she sold to him didn't pay an advance. So with her venture into the song-selling business being somewhat unproductive, she set sail for England on the *Mauritania*.

Shortly after returning from the States she was having dinner with her friend Ben Williams. Ben was a property developer whom she'd been very good to in the past. He'd only been a jobbing builder when Dot asked him to renovate St Mary's Mount. The money she'd paid him had helped to start a very successful building business, resulting in him becoming a millionaire. During the evening it came out that Dot was in financial difficulties and couldn't afford the upkeep of St Mary's Mount. Ben, seeing Dorothy's dilemma, suggested that he convert the servant's quarters of her house into flats; it was the least he could do for the kindness she'd shown him in the past and it would at least earn her some much-needed funds. It turned out to be a shrewd move; the income from the flats gave Dorothy the financial security to keep her beloved home.

At the time Dorothy was, in her words, being bombarded by Roger's solicitors to swear affidavits as to her means. Roger had made a list of what she was purported to be earning. Included on the list was the rent she was earning from the six converted flats at St Mary's Mount. This she thought added insult to injury; not only had he left her for a younger woman but he was trying, as most people do, to pay as little maintenance as possible. She was furious and her reply was both confrontational and accusatory:

Dear Roger,

I have been bombarded by your Solicitors to swear affidavits as to my means; you had made a list of what I was purported to be earning etc., one item intrigued me, rents of the 6 flats in my home St Mary's Mount. There were 22 rooms in St Mary's Mount not including the lodge, 2 large stables and 2 garages, which originally were the chauffer's quarters. When you flew to Hollywood to commence your 2-year contract with M.G.M. at $350 a week for 9 months but your agent had M.G.M. pay pro rata for 52 weeks after various studio deductions net, varied from $150 to $175 per week, out of which we rented our apartment and new furniture to be bought on the time plan so I would not expect you to send any money home to Dada for the upkeep of St Mary's Mount. It was 5 weeks before I could join you in any event due to my outstanding contracts. I discussed my situation with Ben and he suggested I turn a wing into 6 flat-lets, which he had his workmen do. They were beautiful; kitchen units, cookers and sinks in every one, 2 toilets, huge *bathroom and their own private entrance and telephone in the hall.*

It was originally the servants' quarters, the rents were £3.10s a week, alas not enough to cover the upkeep of St Mary's Mount taking into account a maid, Gertrude and a gardener to help my Father, and don't forget Roger, your parents still enjoyed their long weekends at my home.

Eventually the issue was resolved, Roger was ordered to pay maintenance and the flats turned out to be a successful venture. The money she earned from them enabled Dorothy to purchase another property in Erith. This she converted herself. She was very artistic; she did the entire interiors herself; painting walls, upholstering chairs and constructing breakfast bars. She often said in another life she would have loved to have been an interior designer. It would have been no use asking Ben to do the design; he was a great builder but he had no taste – he had a pink house with plastic crabs on the wall, which vied for position with what his wife Robina called a 'Muriel'.

Dorothy used most of what was left of her savings on renovating the properties and had to live on the £4,000-a-year maintenance that the court had ordered Roger to pay her. Ironically for the cash-strapped Dot she had to pay surtax on it, which in those days was 90p in the pound. With what was left of her alimony and the rents from her properties, she was able to stay at Bexley and keep up appearances – very important in the world of show business. It's the only business in the world where one puts one's self up to be knocked down and believe me they love to kick you when you're down, and boy did Dorothy get a kicking.

Dorothy continued to live the film star lifestyle to the full but the money soon ran out. Swallowing her pride, she decided to contact her old friend Bert, who now lived in Port Talbot, South Wales. The working men's club scene was really taking off there and Dorothy was hoping that Bert could fix her a few gigs. Bert was apprehensive; he told her it was crummy work and they didn't pay her kind of money. The going rate for acts in those days was only about £15 a night but he said he would see what he could do.

Bert had a lot of contacts in the Welsh club scene. He was in demand as an accompanist because he was one of the few who could read music, which was more than could be said of many of the so-called club organists; they couldn't read the bloody *Echo* let alone music. If you gave a handwritten manuscript to any of these buskers they would invariably ask for a copy with the pictures on the front so they could follow the words that were printed under the notation.

Bert scoured the South Wales Valleys trying to sell Dorothy. The concert secretaries of the clubs weren't sure if their members would pay enough cover charge to cover her fee but Bert persevered with the hard sell and managed to get her £50 a spot. By fixing her an early gig at a working men's club and a late night gig in a night club he doubled her fee to £100 a night; in two weeks she made £1,400, a lot of money in 1965. Her first gig was at the Bay View Social in Aberavon. The working men's clubs weren't what Dorothy had been used to in her heyday; many of them looked as if they hadn't seen a lick of paint since the general strike. Adorning the walls of these Victorian institutions were large wooden plaques, listing past club chairmen in fading gold paint, photos of past club heroes: rugby players, pigeon fanciers, whippet owners, posters announcing the next rugby international and forthcoming attractions, all stuck on haphazardly with sticky tape. Opposite the entrance, the ubiquitous doorman would sit at his table signing people in, wearing the uniform of all such doormen: cloth cap, three-piece suit, trousers kept up with belt and braces and well polished best boots.

When Dorothy arrived she looked up at the grey uninviting edifice with apprehension, and sighed: 'Come on Bert, let's get this fucking show on the road.' The huge concert hall was full to bursting, but the only sound was the drone of the bingo being called by a dapper MC in a too-tight tuxedo. Someone yelled 'House!' and the place erupted into life. Orders were called, bottles clinked, tills rang. As Dorothy entered with Bert and I carrying her dresses and music, heads turned in recognition and calls of 'Hiya Dot' rang in our ears as we pushed our way through the crowd to get to the dressing room.

Dorothy changed into her beautiful Douggie Darnell gown and gazed apprehensively around the cold unwelcoming dressing room. The photos of semi-pro club turns, stuck on the nicotine-stained walls, were the only decoration. She reflected, as she listened to the hullabaloo going on around her: people ordering drinks, going to the toilet etc., that this was a far cry from the Moulin Rouge in Hollywood. The MC eventually settled the audience down and Dorothy made her entrance. The crowd went wild. She looked around at the expectant faces.

They fell silent. Then a solitary voice from the audience yelled: 'Welcome home Dot!' Dorothy's eyes filled with tears and for an uncomfortable moment I thought she'd forgotten her opening song. Was this déjà vu? The first gig that Bert had been instrumental in getting her all those years ago had started the same way. But pro that she was, she regained her composure and smiling through her tears she sailed into 'Say It With Flowers'. The house rose like magic – Dorothy was home.

In general Dorothy was well received but the last gig at the Maes-y Cymer Rugby Club was a different story. The evening didn't get off to the greatest of starts; a reporter from the BBC had come to interview Dot before the show and whilst she was being interviewed the Concert Sec, who was about as sensitive as a rubber cosh, came into the dressing room and went into the toilet. The peeing perpetrator could be heard from outside. When he came out Dorothy went for him big time. 'You ignorant prick,' she yelled, 'Didn't you know I was doing an interview for the radio?' The bolshie Concert Sec protested that he had to pee somewhere. Dorothy, incensed by his insensitivity, told him he should have pissed on the side like she has to. Suitably chastised, he beat a hasty retreat.

Dorothy made her entrance to sparse applause. Any elation she'd felt from the welcome she'd received at her last gig was soon forgotten; this time the audience was positively hostile. It was obvious that they'd come for the bingo and weren't interested in some 'has-been singer'. Sitting in the front row, a couple of smart arse drunks were giving Dorothy a hard time. The MC, sensing things could turn ugly, grabbed the microphone unceremoniously from Dorothy and called for order. Dorothy, losing her rag, snatched the microphone back, called them a lot of fucking sheep and stormed off the stage. She burst into the dressing room, ripped off her stage frock and started pulling on her street clothes. Bert asked her what the hell she thought she was doing: 'The people out there have paid for their tickets and want to hear you sing!' 'If you think I'm walking out through that bunch of bastards you've got another think coming,' she said, 'I've had it with this place as far as I'm concerned it's over and fucking out; I'm going out the window.' Bert watched in disbelief as Dorothy pulled a chair towards a small fanlight, clambered onto a chair and attempted to climb out of the window, feet first. Ernie her pianist just shrugged; he'd seen it all before. Dorothy was half in/ half out of the fanlight when she slipped. Her descent was halted by the gusset of her knickers, which got caught on the spike of the fanlight and she was left dangling in mid-air like a rag doll. The flimsy material of her knickers couldn't take the strain for long and gave way, resulting in her landing on all fours in the car park. An amiable passing drunk, noticing Dorothy, arse shining in the moonlight, quipped, 'Never mind that lot, *Rosemary*, I thought you were great!' Dorothy, knees grazed and knickers torn yelled, 'My name's Dorothy you prick … now fuck off.'

Heavy winter rain was bouncing off the bonnet of the car as Ernie drove us back to Bert's flat in Aberavon. The atmosphere was frosty to say the least. Breaking the silence, Bert told Dorothy that she had no right to walk off – he didn't care if they were noisy, they'd paid to see her and she owed it to him to give it her best shot. 'If you want to fuck up your own reputation,' he said, 'that's up to you but don't fuck up mine … people know me around here.'

Dorothy, stung by Bert's criticism, screamed for Ernie to stop the car. He pulled over and, oblivious of the wind whipping the rain along the sea front in gusting sheets, she leaped out and proceeded to walk the rest of the way in her dangerously high-heeled shoes. She was drenched; her short blond hair was stuck to her head and her mink coat looked like a drowned rat. Ernie was driving at walking pace, alongside the bedraggled Dorothy and Bert was yelling out of the window: 'Get back into the car. What do you think this is a star is fucking born?' Reluctantly, Dorothy got in and sat there dripping, silent and sullen as Ernie continued on towards Bert's flat.

The next morning Bert, my mother Merville and I were having breakfast when Dorothy entered looking very sheepish. She gave Bert a kiss, said she was sorry for last night and promised it wouldn't happen again – she wouldn't do anything to upset her lovely Bert. Bert said he understood why she'd walked off, they were a bunch of ignorant bastards but he'd worked his arse off getting the gigs. He *had* warned her that it wouldn't be easy but at least she was earning. Dorothy opened her handbag and tipped a pile of screwed up bank notes onto the floor. She flattened them out and started to count. When she got to £1,400 Bert quipped that it wasn't bad for two weeks' work. Grabbing a bunch of notes, she unceremoniously stuffed them into Bert's hand. 'For the commission,' she said. Bert pushed the money back, telling her that he didn't want any commission; he did it to help her: 'After all, what are friends for?' Brandishing the notes she said, 'I'll chuck them into the fucking fire if you don't take them.' Bert was adamant that her need was greater than his; the bills had been piling up since Roger had left. Then, without warning, Dot flung the bunch of fivers into the grate. Bert was gobsmacked, called her a stupid bugger and proceeded to frantically pull the burning fivers out of the fire with his bare hands and stamp the flames out on the mat. Calming down, she said he was right; she could use the money to cut a few demos: 'Perhaps I can persuade Decca to record me again. God knows Dick Rowe owes me a few favours.' It was ironic that the Wales she turned her back on all those years ago had now come to her rescue. She'd returned to her roots and the few crummy gigs she'd done in the Working Men's clubs were the impetus she needed to start her comeback.

She spoke to Decca and persuaded them to make a live album and where better to record it than back in her hometown of Llanelli. The Glen Ballroom, which was once the cinema where Dorothy had marvelled at Al Jolson on the silver screen as a child, was booked for the live performance. She contacted her old friend and pianist Ernie Dunstal and with Michael Barclay, a record producer from Decca, they set about routining her new act.

The act was an emotional rollercoaster, based on the story of Dot's life. The highs and the lows reflected the euphoria when she was riding high with Billy Reid, her time in Hollywood with Roger, which she swears was the happiest she'd ever been, and the despair she felt when he abandoned her for the younger and more beautiful Luisa. The show was a triumph; the audience gave her a 10-minute ovation. Llanelli and Wales had welcomed Dorothy back with open arms and at the end of the show they stood as one and sang 'We'll Keep a Welcome in the Hillside'. With tears coursing down her face she thanked them and promised that this was only the beginning; she was back and she would never desert them again.

The following week Dorothy hired Decca Studios and a thirty-piece orchestra. Keith Miller was on keyboards and Nicky Welch did the arrangements and produced the session. Los Zafiros and I were asked to do the vocals on two of the new songs she'd written and Dot recorded the rest. I was over the moon; I'd never recorded before and she told me that if the demos turned out well it might lead to me getting a recording contract. She'd spun the same story to Los Zafiros so we did the session for nothing. The large studio orchestra was assembled. Some of the blasé string players were reading newspapers; they'd seen it all before. Others were chatting waiting to start. Dorothy was discussing her routine with Nicky her musical director when she noticed Trevor, the engineer, with head in hands looking decidedly worse for wear. It turned out that the poor sod had the flu. Dorothy rummaged about in her bag and came up with a small purple tablet and gave it to him. 'What's this?' he said, 'Will it cure my flu?' 'No,' she said, 'but you won't give a fuck if you've got the flu or not!' Nicky quipped that it was no wonder they called her 'Pusher Squires'. All the musicians, who were listening to the conversation on the fold-back, cracked up laughing. Dorothy laid down her tracks first, followed by Los Zafiros and then me. The session went on into the early hours of the morning and Nicky was getting a bit edgy. He was an alcoholic and his hip flask was empty so Dorothy rang Tony Osborne, another celebrated composer and arranger, for replenishments. Tony had been the arranger on her last hit 'Say It With Flowers'. Ironically, he was now Shirley Bassey's musical director, Dorothy's biggest rival, and was responsible for writing the arrangement of one of Shirley's biggest hits – 'I Who Have Nothing'.

Tony lived in a beautiful house in a circular drive with a small roundabout in the middle. It had started to snow when I arrived; the whole thing looked like a Christmas card. Tony answered the door and handed me a bottle of whiskey called Hanky Bannister. When I took it back to the studio, Nicky wasn't too impressed. 'What the fuck's this?' he said squinting at the bottle, 'It sounds like a fucking long distant runner.' It wasn't his usual Crawford's Five Star single malt but he drank it anyway and the session continued. It was getting very late by now and I was last to record. The song was called 'One More Chance'. Dorothy gave me a real hard time; she said I didn't have the right feel. I don't know why she didn't record it herself; I'm sure it was a love song to Roger. However, after numerous takes she was happy, the session was wrapped up and we went looking for somewhere to eat. It was three o'clock in the morning and the only place open was a transport cafe populated by long-distance lorry drivers and taxi drivers. Heads turned as Dorothy, in mink coat and diamante glasses, surrounded by her entourage, entered the cafe. Dorothy, high on adrenaline from the recording session, was holding court. When a man in a dirty white apron plonked cheese on toast in front of her she asked if he had any chutney. Nicky, seeing the funny side retorted, 'Where do you think you are The Savoy? You'll be asking for bleedin' ketchup next.' Dorothy, brandishing the master tape she's just cut, countered, 'We'll be *eating* at The Savoy when these songs come out; they're gonna be a fucking smash!'

The week after the recording session, Dorothy flew to Los Angeles and I, along with Jason the dog and May the housekeeper, were left to house sit, with strict instructions to open any mail that came and to let her know immediately of any news from Decca. I was awoken one morning by a large bulky envelope landing with a thud amongst the bills and junk mail on the floor. The label read 'Fragile – Records'. I think Dot must have had a sixth sense because she phoned from LA that morning and asked if she'd received anything. I told her of the package from Decca and she told me to open it. I tore it open and found it to be the demos we had cut the week before. The compliment slip had one short sentence turning all the songs down. I was as disappointed as Dot by this news; I was hoping to get a recording contract out of it. But all was not lost; by the strangest of coincidences I received a phone call that morning from Tony Saxon, the brother of Al Saxon, the singer. Tony had been a bit of an agent who'd booked me a couple of gigs in the past. He told me he was now working for President Records and they were looking for a male singer and did I have any demos. I told him that as it happened I had the demo from Decca with a thirty-piece orchestra backing me. So an appointment was made for me to meet the boss of President Records, Eddie Kassner.

Why I'm telling you all this is because the meeting with Eddie was intrinsically linked to the rest of Dot's recording career.

8

President Records

I climbed the rickety stairs that led to Eddie Kassner's office. Sat behind reception was Jenny Howells, a pretty blonde girl with a skirt so short you could see what she'd had for breakfast. She nodded me towards Eddie's office. It looked like the headquarters of the SMERCH. Eddie, a short, fat East European Jewish gentleman sitting behind an enormous leather-topped desk, a fat cigar protruding from his mouth, looked like he'd been sent from Central Casting. Stood next to him was a beautiful German girl half his age, euphemistically referred to as his girlfriend. Next to her was a record producer he'd poached from EMI and Keith Mansfield, a musical arranger who'd been instrumental in the success of a group called Love Affair.

Eddie was ruthless. He told me he didn't like the song Dorothy had penned. He liked my voice, however, and would sign me on condition that I wasn't signed to Dorothy. I told him that I'd never been signed to anyone; the only reason I had done the demo for Dot was so that she could sell the songs to Decca. So, we shook hands, the deal was done and Eddie told me he would find me a song that would do for me what 'Portrait of My Love' had done for Matt Monroe. Then, turning to Keith Mansfield, he said, 'I want you to do a great arrangement for Johnny; I don't care how much you spend on musicians but I don't want glockenspiel, one note fifteen fucking quid'.

When Dorothy returned from LA and found that I'd been signed to Eddie Kassner's label, she hit the roof. She rang Eddie and demanded to know what the hell he was doing poaching her artist. The next day I received a phone call from Eddie wanting to know what the hell was going on. I reiterated that I wasn't signed to anyone and that Dorothy had never mentioned being my manager. Eddie accepted my explanation and I duly signed a three-single deal with President Records. Dorothy wasn't happy but the ever-streetwise Dot turned the situation to her advantage. Eddie, cigar in hand, was sitting behind his desk when Dorothy, armed with her demos, stormed unannounced into his office. She told him that what he had done was sharp practice and all but blackmailed him into recording her as well. Not an easy thing to do; Eddie was one of the sharpest guys in the business – he hadn't escaped Nazi Germany and become a millionaire for nothing.

Dorothy proceeded to give him the hard sell, telling him that she'd already paid for the recording session so what did he have to lose. 'For Christ sake,' she cajoled, 'just press a few thousand copies, my fan base will guarantee thousands of sales from my concerts alone. They'll be a fucking smash I know they will.' Eddie wasn't convinced, he had great respect for Dorothy as an artist but he wasn't sure that her kind of material would sell. Dorothy continued to haggle as only she could; I'm sure Dot would have made a great agent if only she could have left her ego as a performer behind. She insisted that he was making a big mistake; she was still hot. After pondering the situation, Eddie capitulated and said he would record her on one condition, that she would record one of his songs. Dorothy, scenting victory, seized the opportunity and agreed but only if she could have one of her songs on the B-side. It's not generally known but the writer of the B-side gets the same royalties as the writer of the A-side – there were no flies on Dorothy. Eddie smiled. They shook hands. And the deal was struck.

Dorothy had a few hits on President Records: 'For Once In my Life,' 'Till' and 'My Way' all got in the charts. But when she decided to record 'My Way' everybody thought she was mad. She went to The White Lion before the session. The pub was full of the Tin Pan Alley crowd, songwriters and musicians. Dot was in full flow, telling anyone who'd listen that she was going to record 'My Way'. One wag quipped, 'In case you haven't heard Dot, Sinatra is in the charts with it already.' Dorothy in full flight said, 'I'll sing the arse off Sinatra; you just watch me.' And true to her word, she recorded it and it got in the charts but she had hell's own job convincing the BBC to play it. Dorothy decided to confront Doreen Davies, the producer of the *Jimmy Young Show*, the biggest show on the air at the time. Because of its huge audience it almost guaranteed entry into the charts. She drove her Chrysler Barracuda to the BBC offices at Aeolian Hall in Bond Street, parked the car on a double yellow line, opened the glove compartment, which was crammed with unpaid parking tickets, took one out, and tucked it under the windscreen wiper. She used this ploy all the time but she didn't fool the traffic wardens, she always ended up with another ticket. It didn't make any difference; she never paid them anyway.

I was at Bexley when a police officer called and asked to see Dot about her outstanding tickets. I told him to wait and went in search of Dot. I told her there was a policeman outside. She told me to tell him she was in the bath, which I did. 'I'll come back later,' he said with a wry smile. When he returned she told me to tell him she was out to which he quipped, 'That was a quick bath ... Just tell her that her favourite policeman called.' Anyway, back to the plot.

Dorothy confronted Doreen Davies, demanding to know why the BBC wasn't playing her records. Doreen said she understood Dorothy's frustration – she had nothing against her as an artist but she had to understand that her records weren't on the BBC playlist so she couldn't play them; it was as simple as that. Dorothy protested that 'My Way' had been in the charts for six months to which Doreen replied, 'but not the BBC charts.' Dorothy accused her of being part of a conspiracy. 'I'm in the charts,' she yelled, 'How the hell can I get on the playlist if you bastards won't play it?' It was a catch-22 situation.

When Dorothy returned home that night I was in the library. It was my favourite room in the whole house, a kind of sanctuary if you like.

The peaceful book-lined room had an open fire, which I had just lit and the chattering flames of a log fire were reflected on the wine-red walls. I had just opened a book when Dorothy stormed in, shattering the peace. She kicked off her shoes and stood legs planted firmly apart in a defiant stance. 'What have I got to do to prove myself, John?' she demanded. 'I've been in the charts for fifteen months with the last three singles. Christ … "My Way" has been in the charts for six months and *still* that bastard Jimmy Young won't play it.' She suddenly stopped her rant. Then, looking very vulnerable, she whispered, 'I wouldn't care, John, but I'm only a little fella.'

Dorothy didn't give up. Local radio stations had opened all over the country so, determined to beat the monopoly of the BBC, Dorothy drove up and down the country doing interviews at every local radio station on route. It was hard work; she would be working three clubs a night. Then, with Hilda, her secretary, she would drive to the local stations taking her records with her. She covered probably eight in a day, which reached about half a million listeners. After covering all of them she would drive back to do her three shows. Her hard work paid off and after covering thousands of miles 'My Way' entered the BBC charts.

I moved out of St Mary's Mount a few weeks later and didn't see Dorothy for some time. I'd been poached by Southern Music who had just launched their own record label Spark Records. Dorothy stayed with President Records and the next time we met up was in Gibraltar. Bob Kingston, my recording manager, had submitted some of my demos to the Gibraltar Song Festival and I was chosen to represent Britain with a song called 'Don't Take Your Love Away', a song Bob had penned with Geoff Stephens of *Winchester Cathedral* fame. There had been a lot of trouble with the Spanish demanding Gibraltar be part of Spain at the time but there was still a strong feeling of Britishness in the protectorate so it was suggested that it would be a good idea to include a patriotic song at the festival to boost morale.

So a special Gibraltar Anthem was commissioned for the festival and the composers, Brian Willie and Ronnie Bridges, asked Dorothy to sing it. Brian remembers:

I asked Dorothy to perform it, she said she would and duly did so, on Saturday 14 November 1970, in St Michaels Cave in Gibraltar. The venue may sound strange, but it is actually a magnificent natural 500-seat auditorium, halfway up the Rock, resplendent with stalactites and stalagmites as a backdrop. It was a very exciting occasion especially for me because the anthem was so well received that night; Dorothy had to Encore it twice.

The festival was a fantastic experience. Fifteen songs were chosen to be sung and I was to sing for Britain. Just before I went on, Dorothy advised me, no … she instructed me, not to use the hand Mic. 'Don't run around like a headless chicken,' she scolded, 'stand at the microphone and command your audience.' It was alien to me, I'd always been used to using a hand microphone, but I bowed to greater experience. Dorothy was right as usual; I did what I was told and won the contest. All the singers had to sing three times, after the first rendition five were dropped and ten of us had to sing again. This was then whittled down to the final three. A beautiful girl called Rosanella Loveband, who used to sing on a radio show called *Parade of the Pops*, had two songs in the contest; they were both belters and Rosa was a great singer.

I was convinced that Rosa would win it; I thought I might be lucky enough to come second. I waited backstage, biting my nails, waiting for the result when I was aware of someone trying to get my attention in the wings – it was Dorothy. 'You've got it,' she said in a stage whisper, 'I've just seen the judge's scores. By the way what are you doing on the 6 December?' 'Nothing much,' I replied. 'You are now,' she said with a smile, 'You'll be supporting me on the Palladium.' I couldn't believe my luck, all I could do was croak thank you, which seemed a bit inadequate; the Palladium was the most famous theatre in the world. 'I could never have survived in show business if your father hadn't done what he did for me,' she said, 'That's why I'm putting you on.' Then as a passing shot she said, 'I hope you've got some big arrangements, I'm using a thirty-piece orchestra.' After hitting me with that bombshell she kissed me then, leaving me in a state of euphoria, made her entrance like the demon king in that stalagmite-encrusted cave to give a rip-roaring encore of the Gibraltar Anthem.

The winner's party was held for me at the Rock Hotel. Dorothy arrived with Jack Dabbs, the producer of *Four Way Family Favourites*. I was sat with Bob Kingston, my recording manager and my ex-wife, when Jack came over. He told Bob, if he could get a copy of my song to him he would give it a plug on his programme.

When he left, Dorothy approached and alluding to Jack Dabbs said, 'That bastard is even putting his fags on my bill.' I found out later that Dot was paying for all Jack's expenses. I'll never forget Sunday 6 December 1970, not only because I was to appear with Dot at the Palladium, but also, that day I was expecting to hear my record played on *Family Favourites*, as Jack had promised. As I drove to London, radio blaring, Don Durbidge's familiar voice came over the airwaves, announcing *Four Way Family Favourites*. Don linked up with Judith Chalmers and related the events of the Gibraltar Festival. I waited expectantly for my plug. You can imagine my disappointment when, instead of introducing my record, he played Dorothy singing 'My Way'.

Although I could never prove it, I'm sure she'd got Jack to play her record instead of mine. Who's to say I wouldn't have done the same thing, given the opportunity. Showbiz is a 'dog eat dog' business. The difference between bribery and inducement is a fine line; businessmen take clients out for lunch all the time. But in the sixties and seventies there was a culture of giving inducements to producers and disc jockeys to play records on high-profile programmes. Dorothy would live to regret inviting Jack to Gibraltar; a big scandal was about to erupt in the press and Dorothy was the main protagonist.

Before the story broke, Dorothy had had a meeting with Bernard Delfont at London Management regarding a future booking at the Palladium. Bernard didn't think she would do the business on her own; it had been a long time since she'd topped the bill at any London venue, so he offered her a date sharing the bill with Danny La Rue. Dorothy was furious. She insisted that she was still a draw; she'd been packing them in all over the country and she wasn't about to share the bill with anyone, not even Danny. Danny was a very big friend of Dot's; he always said he learnt a lot from her.

Dorothy accused Bernard Delfont of being influenced by Roger Moore; he was also represented by the Delfont office and she'd convinced herself that it was all Roger's doing. She said it was killing him to see her making it again. In my opinion, the only reason she was making the comeback was in the misguided hope that Roger would come back to her. In truth I don't think he had given her comeback a second thought. He was happy with Luisa and his children. After turning Delfont's offer down she decided to go it alone. She was driving down the Old Kent Road to Bexley, when she had an epiphany, 'The hell with it!' she yelled, slapping the dashboard, 'I'm going to book the Palladium myself.'

The last time she'd played the Palladium was on one of Ted Gollup's celebrity concerts. Ted Gollup was the booker and wanted Dorothy to go on first spot. She hit the roof. 'The hell I am,' she said 'put Anne Shelton or somebody else in that spot. I'm not going to do it and that's it.' Ted was always doing this to Dot; if he wanted someone to fill in he knew he could rely on her to do a good job. Ted pleaded with her not to let him down and after a lot of haggling she relented. A lot of stars had to follow her that night, which turned out not to be an easy task; she sang three numbers and brought the house down. It was fortuitous that she'd done the first spot for Ted that night, because now he owed her a favour and she was determined to call it in:

I went straight to Eddie Kassner's office and asked Roger Bolton, one of his A&R men, if I could use his phone and I called Ted Gollup. I said, 'Ted I want to book the Palladium.' I took the worst date imaginable: 6 December. Nobody books a date in December, it's too near Christmas. Ted said you're not putting a group on are you? No I said it's for me you Twerp. One or two shows he said? I said one show. I asked how much it was. Well … when he told me the price I thought, oh blimey now I've done it; I didn't sleep all weekend. He called me on the Monday at my office in Oxford Street and confirmed the date. There was no going back now. The next day I arrived for the press conference; Mike Housego, who was one of the greatest press guys in the country, ordered all the champagne and I made all the hors d'oeuvres. I thought there would be about a dozen there, you know? When I got there it was like a football match. They were shoving microphones under my nose.

The Evening Standard and *The Star* photographed me walking down Argyle Street and at half past five the following morning they [the audience] were all queuing up. It was incredible.

La Squires was a Spice Girl ahead of her time. She was a woman in a man's world; she showed she was as good as any man when it came to business.

9

The Bill For The First Palladium Concert

After the deal was struck Dorothy began her preparations for her comeback. She was like Rocky, getting ready for the main event, jogging for miles and doing fifty to a hundred sit-ups a day. She relentlessly rehearsed her 2-hour show with her new pianist Kenny Brown, until she was word perfect. Kenny was a good pianist but secretly she was hoping Keith would come back. A week or two before the show, we were in The White Lion and Keith was there. Dorothy made a beeline for him and tried to get him to agree to play on the forthcoming concert. She offered him double the money but Dot wasn't fooling anyone, she was trying to get Keith back not only as a pianist but as a lover. Keith wasn't falling for it. He said no and no amount of money would make him change his mind, although, he could have done with it – he was playing in a Southwark pub at the time. Keith had his principles and he was sticking to them.

That part of her life over, Dorothy threw herself into preparing for the comeback of her life. She hadn't had a great education, having left school at 15, but she had a natural flare and she certainly knew her business when it came to producing a show. She arranged everything that night at the Palladium:

producing, directing and even booking the musicians. Dorothy's stagecraft was boundless; she'd learnt the hard way by putting on variety shows and pantomimes in the provinces. When Roger Moore played the King in one of Dorothy's pantomimes, Emily's mother, Joyce Golding, who was in the show, remembered the band playing a practical joke on Roger. They switched his glass of water for one of gin and when it came to his big number they played the song in the wrong key. It ended Roger's singing career, long before he crashed out of a Lloyd Webber production of *Aspects of Love*.

When the press announced that Dorothy had hired the Palladium to stage her own show, the talk on the street was that she would need Tom Jones on the bill to fill such a large auditorium. But she was to prove them all wrong. The cynics hadn't accounted for her vast army of fans who'd been loyal throughout her career and the 2,200-seat theatre was sold out within a couple of hours. There were people queuing around the block. Mounted police were holding back the crowds. Even the press had to buy their own tickets. Edwin Shaw, the production co-ordinator for Lloyd Webber's theatres, was the box office manager at the Palladium at the time and remembers Dorothy's comeback show vividly and was quoted as saying:

> Dorothy came to see me about ticketing and asked what prices she should charge. She was a bit nervous, she knew if she didn't get it right she could end up with just a few fans in the huge auditorium. She could have charged rock bottom prices but she went with the going rate. She got it just right; even the infamous ticket tout, Stan Flashman, had difficulty getting extra tickets.

I'll never forget being part of that fantastic occasion; the whole day is indelibly etched on my memory. That afternoon the stage was packed with musicians, backing singers and supporting artists waiting to rehearse. Johnny Gray, a saxophonist and sought-after session musician, augmented the thirty-piece orchestra and backed Dorothy on her version of 'My Way', Simon Oates and Pete Murray were there to link the show and my old mate Stan Stennett was there to provide the comedy. While I waited my turn to rehearse, I watched Dorothy, sitting on a stool, in headscarf and dark glasses while Nicky

Welch took her through her new musical arrangements, and marvelled at the enormity of what she was about to achieve.

After she'd finished doing her band call she told me I would be closing the first half of the show. I thanked her for giving me the chance to perform on that iconic stage; after all this was the Palladium, the most famous theatre in the world. She told me that she was being offered £500 a time by agents to put their artist on the bill, just so they could then say that their artists had played the Palladium. 'I wouldn't do it,' she said, 'I'm doing it for you for what your father did for me. But be under no illusion, John. I wouldn't put you on if you were no fucking good.' Then she kissed me, told me to break a leg and quipped, 'but not when you're tap dancing.'

I'd fallen foul of the Lord Chamberlain at rehearsals; as soon as I started to tap dance, Ted Gollup, who was stage managing, ran onto the stage yelling, 'you can't do that.' In those days there was a ridiculous rule forbidding anyone to dance in any theatre on a Sunday. I knew this but thought I could get away with it. Dot had a word with Ted. I don't know what she said but Ted turned a blind eye to my indiscretion and I was allowed to include the tap routine in my act. The time of the curtain arrived. I stood nervously in the wings waiting to go on. The orchestra stuck up my intro and I made my entrance. The atmosphere was fantastic. The audience was very receptive and I finished my spot to warm applause but I was under no illusion, they were all really waiting for Dorothy. When I went to Dot's dressing room to wish her luck there was a crisis going on; Dorothy, dressed only in her bra and knickers, was pacing up and down screaming blue murder – Douggie Darnell hadn't arrived with her new gown for the performance and she was refusing to go on without it. Hilda Brown, Dot's secretary, was trying to persuade her to wear another dress but she wasn't having any of it. 'It's bad luck,' she screamed, 'I'll fucking kill him.' Hilda told her that she would have to wear another dress; they couldn't hold the curtain any longer. Dorothy turned to Pete Murray and told him to get out there and pad it out. Pete was at a loss for words, 'What'll I tell 'em?' he spluttered, to which Dot unceremoniously replied, 'Any fuckin' thing … Tell 'em a joke.' Pete's protestations that he wasn't a comic fell on deaf ears and Dorothy went on with her tirade, 'I paid two fuckin' grand for that gown,' she screamed 'and I'm not going on without it – where is that whoremaster?' Douggie was in a taxi, stuck in traffic frantically sewing beads onto the flamboyant gown of silk and ostrich feathers. The tension backstage was tangible. Nobody was quite sure what to do. Pete Murray was on stage ad-libbing and trying his best to entertain the audience, who were starting to get restless. Dorothy was getting really paranoid. 'I wouldn't put it past those bastards to have fuckin kidnapped Douggie,' she yelled, 'They've tried everything else to stop me.' Who *they* were was anybody's guess.

At last Douggie arrived. He was fighting his way through the melee of musicians and backstage staff when Dorothy spotted him. She grabbed the dress and started to pull it on, demanding to know where the fuck he'd been. Douggie tried to explain, while zipping her up, that he'd been stuck in traffic. Ignoring his feeble excuse, she looked at her reflection in the full-length mirror; the dress, of purple silk with a chiffon bolero trimmed with ostrich feathers, was magnificent, if a bit over the top. Dot looked a million dollars. Softening, she kissed him and said: 'It's bloody marvellous, Douggie but don't think you're off the hook yet … I'll bloody sort you out later.' Pete's patter was drying up. He looked nervously towards the wings and seeing Dorothy was ready to make her entrance, a relieved Pete started to make his announcement: 'Well … I don't know what to say about this lady she's …' With that, a fan yelled, 'She's wonderful' and the audience exploded into spontaneous applause. Spasmodic voices from the audience continued to yell encouragement. Pete was waiting patiently for the audience to settle down when someone shouted: 'Bring her on.' It was all Pete could do to complete his introduction. When he eventually announced 'Ladies and Gentlemen, Miss Dorothy Squires,' the auditorium erupted. As Dorothy made her entrance the whole audience rose as one and gave her a 5-minute standing ovation. Overcome by emotion, she just stood, tears in her eyes. It had been a long, hard climb back to the top and everything depended on that night. She raised her hand, and one by one, the audience fell silent.

In a hoarse whisper she said, 'I hope I remember it all'. Then a lone fan yelled, 'You will, Dot. You will.' The atmosphere was tear jerking, a real lump in the throat moment. There was a long pause; for a minute it looked as if she'd dried then, Kenny played an arpeggio and Dorothy sailed into 'Everything Is Beautiful'.

I stood watching Dot's incredible performance from the wings. For the next 2 hours Dorothy wrung every ounce of emotion from her performance. As she hit the last note of 'My Way', the audience rose again to give her another standing ovation and shower the stage with flowers. Then, with tears flowing, she exited stage left and started yelling excitedly and uncontrollably, into my face: 'Did you see their fuckin' faces John? Did you see their fuckin' faces?' The subtext to that outburst was that she'd done it; she'd defied the doubting Thomases – Dorothy was back. Then with adrenaline pumping she turned on her heels and re-entered for her encore. I lost count how many curtain calls she took but the audience was still yelling for more when the safety curtain was flown in. The stage was strewn with flowers, thrown by her adoring fans. Presents of every description were handed over the footlights not least a magnum of Moët and Chandon champagne from her great friend Danny La Rue.

Later, in her dressing room, fellow artists, reporters from the National Press and family and friends, vied for space with well-wishers. The champagne flowed like water. Dorothy was so high I thought she would never come down. Amongst the crowd was John Lloyd, the sports writer for the *Daily Express*. He was Dorothy's biggest fan and later became the president of her fan club. I'd first met John when I'd been working at the Celebrity Restaurant. He particularly liked my wicked impression of Dot with wig and eyelashes and the next day I received a letter from him written in green ink saying how much he'd enjoyed my show. I told Dot about it. She was intrigued; *she'd* been getting the same kind of letters, always in green ink but always anonymous. Pointing him out, I told her that he was the guy who wrote to us in green ink. Dorothy had known John Lloyd for years and was surprised to know that he was the author of the mysterious letters. She couldn't understand why he hadn't signed them. It was obvious to me why; he was totally in awe of 'La Squires' and too timid to declare his adulation face to face.

When the party finally finished Dorothy and I left by the stage door. If she thought she was going straight home she had another think coming; the fans outside were six deep, clamoring for her autograph. She must have been exhausted but she signed every single one. When the last book was signed George, the stage doorman, yelled: 'You showed 'em Dot; I've seen 'em all here from Shirley to Judy and you topped the lot.' Slipping him a generous tip she said: 'This is just the beginning, George; it'll be a nationwide tour next.'

Dorothy always left very generous tips for the stage doorkeepers, but only if they deserved it. In some cases they could be a bit bolshie; they would be respectful to the headliners but they were not always so courteous to the supporting acts. Dorothy couldn't stand discrimination and always stood up for the underdog:

> The stage doormen couldn't come it with me. When I heard them speaking to the other acts; 'cos I was one of the other acts at one time, I would clean the bastards. I remember playing Birmingham Hippodrome my brother had arrived earlier. I went inside to the stage door keeper. And I asked him if he could get me a couple of stagehands to help me with my baggage. He said get them yourself. So when I finished that week. I said to him, normally, I leave a very generous tip for the stage doorman but you are not getting a penny for the way you spoke to me. I didn't know you were the headliner when you arrived he said. It makes no difference I said whether I was the headliner or not. You don't talk to acts like that however low on the bill they are.

The day after the Palladium, Dot was invited to the Annual Variety Club Ball, which was held in the Great Room at the Dorchester Hotel on Park Lane. For the uninitiated, Variety Club is a charitable organisation that raises money for disadvantaged or disabled children. It was formed after a small baby was left on the steps of the Sheridan Square Film Theatre in Pittsburgh in 1928 with a note that read:

> Please take care of my baby. Her name is Catherine. I can no longer take care of her. I have eight others. My husband is out of work. She was born on

Thanksgiving Day. I have always heard of the goodness of show business people and pray to God that you will look after her.

It was signed, a heartbroken mother.

All the money raised at these events goes to the charity and Dorothy, never one to do things by halves, paid for a table for twenty; no small sum when you think the tickets can cost £100 and more. As she made her entrance down the sweeping staircase the whole room rose as one to give her a standing ovation. It had been a long, hard road back to the top and to have the acknowledgement of her achievement by her peers was the icing on the cake. Unbeknown to her, Roger had booked a table for himself and Luisa. As Dorothy swept past their table, reveling in the plaudits of the crowd, they averted their eyes. Dot pretended not to notice them but she wasn't fooling me. A little later she asked Emily to go with her to the toilet and made sure she went to the one that took her past Roger's table. Roger just lowered his head as she passed with her nose in the air.

These Variety Club events are usually sugary sycophantic soirées. A year earlier, 1969 to be exact, they decided to honour Roger with a lunch for his showbiz achievements and charitable works. The BBC televised it. A lot of backslapping went on as usual with speakers, usually friends, eulogizing profusely on how great he was. These speeches are usually a combination of wit and sarcasm. On the occasion of Roger's tribute, Leslie Bricusse, the renowned composer, gave a speech, which because of its content, referring to Dorothy, was cut out of the broadcast. Later Peter Tory of *The Daily Express* wrote this:

It is typically annoying of the BBC that they should decide to edit out of one of their more sugary showbiz tributes, the only moment of genuine fun and excitement. During The Variety Club Lunch to honour Roger Moore this week, composer Leslie Bricusse observed unwisely; 'Roger has made great sacrifices for popular music – he even married Dorothy Squires.' The remark, said the Corporation, would be struck from last night's BBC1 screening of the event. Mr Bricusse cannot have possibly known the implications of what he was saying. The rest of the audience however did. They shifted uneasily in their seats, some evidently quite fearful, in Cathedral silence. Those who know Welsh singer Miss Squires, indeed, no doubt expecting to hear the shattering of glass above the banqueting hall of London's Hilton and to see the lady in question abseiling down in frogmen's flippers, to lay waste to the top table. She certainly would have read the following morning's newspaper report on Mr Bricusse's joke.

Those of us, who have had any dealings with Miss Squires, a figure who makes the traditional 'woman scorned' look like a whimsical novice nun, know well the consequences of crossing the lady. We all observed in awe, during the post divorce of Mr Moore and Miss Squires, the Celtic rage and fury which ensued. Few of us who chronicled the drama failed to be unsettled by the experience. I recall writing in this newspaper a fairly mild account of Miss Squires' excitable behavior. On the morning of publication I received a call from a distressed woman, evidently Miss Squires' secretary, who shouted down the line: 'Now look what you've done'. Naturally I was unable to see anything at all. However, the lady had held the receiver out into the room for I heard at the other end of the wire the most dreadful carry-on, moaning and groaning and what-have-you.

No, Mr Bricusse cannot have known what he was saying. Small wonder, certainly, that Mr Moore looked as if he had been touched between the shoulder blades by an electric prod. A moment of true television drama denied to us all.

10

The Tour

Dorothy was on a roll now and true to her word, she took the whole show on the road including the full orchestra, manager, publicity agent et al. It was quite an entourage. We covered every major theatre in the country, playing to packed houses wherever we went: Manchester Palace, Liverpool Empire, Bristol Hippodrome, Birmingham Hippodrome, Cardiff Capitol, Newcastle City Hall, Leeds Grand, Brighton Dome and the Royal Albert Hall and so on.

She was now on a quest to conquer the world and on 22 July 1972 she flew to New York to negotiate a date at the Carnegie Hall for her one-woman show. She returned on the *QE2* on 11 August, having secured the date at Carnegie Hall and also a date at the Dorothy Chandler Pavilion in LA, the venue that was used for the Academy Awards, before they started using the new Kodak Theatre.

In her usual over the top fashion, she contacted two gay girls who ran a travel agency. They chartered a jumbo jet for her loyal British fans. The plane was full but apart from their support, the show was not well patronised. It was a step too far. It had been a long time since she'd played America; no one remembered her anymore. Richard Armitage at the Noel Gay Organisation tried to drum up business by trying to sell her as an eccentric like Mrs Millar, the woman who used to hire the Carnegie Hall then sing out of tune. He thought he was doing the right thing but when Dot found out she hit the roof. Mind you her behaviour was becoming increasingly eccentric; she placed a full-page advertisement for a concert in the stage newspaper including several appeals to God and enjoined everyone planning to attend the concert to have bums on seats by 7.30 p.m. sharp in honour of her Britannic Majesty Queen Elizabeth. Needless to say, none of the royal family attended the concert.

As I look back on that time, I remember the great fun we had and the camaraderie of the cast and crew. Apart from the orchestra, Dot travelled Mike Housego, the publicity guy; Bunny Lewis, our agent; Kenny Brown, her pianist; Nicky Welch, her MD; Pancho Villa, a surreal comedian, who dressed and talked like a Mexican, although if you caught him off guard his accent betrayed the fact that he came from Oldham and Tommy Godfrey who compered the show. Tommy was a real 'Cockney Sparrow', who spoke a lot of the time in Cockney rhyming slang. He'd been in a dancing act and according to Dorothy was a very good tap dancer but of late he'd gone into acting in situation comedies. Dorothy, having worked with him in variety, decided to book him to compere the show. Big mistake; apart from the fact he liked a drop of the hard stuff, he was also a gambler. Bunny Lewis, the agent for the show, had been warned not to pay Tommy directly but to pay it directly to Tommy's agent because Tommy would blow the money as soon as he got it and his agent wouldn't get his commission. This was a bone of contention for Tommy who was always asking where Bunny was with his greens – short for green gages – being rhyming slang for wages.

When we arrived at Liverpool Empire it transpired that someone had stolen the flowers, which were traditionally handed up to Dorothy at the end of each show. Tommy, being a little bit pissed decided to get some more. When he returned carrying a bunch of dripping dahlias it was obvious that he'd nicked them from a graveyard. Being three sheets to the wind, he decided to go on stage clutching the bunch of flowers. It was well known in the profession that Dorothy hated an MC to come on stage until she'd taken her last curtain call and she was furious. She whispered something in his ear and Tommy beat a hasty retreat. As he staggered past me in the wings he spluttered: 'She called me a cunt.'

I knew that from that moment on, his days were numbered and after the next concert at Bristol Hippodrome she sacked him. I was standing with him backstage as Dorothy gave her curtain speech: 'I'd like to thank my wonderful musical director Nicky Welch and my wonderful pianist Kenny Brown.'

Tommy, pissed as usual, spluttered, 'Hear that? Nicky Welch, Kenny fucking Brown? Fuck us we're just wines and fucking spirits,' wines and spirits being the last and least significant thing printed on the bill. Then, turning to me he asked who was replacing him. Truthfully, I said I didn't know. To which he said: 'I hope he's a bleedin' good runner – he'll have to be, to catch that Bunny Lewis for his fucking green gages.' I was last out of the theatre that night – well, last except for Nicky Welch. He was totally plastered. Nicky had given the band a right roasting for not pulling their weight at rehearsal so to appease him they all bought him a drink, all thirty of them. As I passed his dressing room I was confronted with the apparition of the inebriated Nicky, swaying precariously back and forth with his trousers around his ankles. I asked him if he was OK to which he replied in his Glaswegian accent, 'Hey son, can ye help me on with me breeks.' I did as I was asked and he staggered out of the stage door, making for the adjacent Indian restaurant, effing and blinding that everybody had gone without him. It was a good job that Jan Leeming, who'd been covering the show for the local newspaper that night, hadn't been witness to this farrago, although, it would have made fascinating reading. After Nicky had gone I went back on stage to collect my music and noticed that not only *my* orchestrations were there but Nicky had forgotten to pick up Dorothy's as well. So I gathered them all and took them to the next gig. If I hadn't, goodness knows how Dorothy would have done her next show; she couldn't have expected a thirty-piece orchestra to busk her entire 2-hour set.

I can't be certain of the order in which we did the concerts; we crisscrossed the country in no logical fashion. We seemed to live on the M6. We would travel from Newcastle to Brighton then back to Manchester then Cardiff and so on. One memorable night I remember was when we played the Pavilion in Glasgow. The Scots are not too keen on English performers, especially comedians, but Dot, being Welsh, always took them by storm. The audience at the Glasgow Pavilion were still yelling for more when the safety curtain had been flown in. Being Glasgow, some of the audience had over imbibed on the old familiar juice and one old bird staggered down the aisle yelling 'Sing Bonnie Mary of Argyle'. Dorothy, not being familiar with it, turned to her MD and whispered 'Play "Coming through the Rye" and leave the last line to me.' When she'd finished the woman looked at her, there was an awkward pause and then she said, 'You're drunker than I am Vera Lynn.'

It was certainly an experience touring with Dorothy and it wasn't without incident. We had just done a concert at the Newcastle City Hall and the next gig happened to be at the Brighton Dome. I didn't fancy driving the 350 miles the following morning and then doing a show. So when the curtain came down, I decided to drive through the night to Brighton. Dorothy was very motherly towards me; she was worried that I would fall asleep at the wheel. After every show she would say, 'Be careful in that bloody sports car of yours.' Knowing what I was intending to do, she insisted I go to see The Doc; he could give me something to keep me awake. I said I didn't think we had a doctor on tour with us. Laughing at my naivety, she told me that Doc was the first violinist. Doc had every pill under the sun. He gave me a black bomber and told me it would help keep me awake for the drive. After the show finished I didn't feel mentally tired but I was physically exhausted so I changed my mind and decided to go the next day. I needn't have bothered, the black bomber kept me awake all night.

I felt like shit the next morning and still had to drive the 350 miles to Brighton. The Brighton Dome was a sell out and, as usual, Dorothy got the customary standing ovation. Dot was very hospitable; after every show there would be drinks for everyone in her dressing room. That particular night, however, Adrian West, a gay friend of Dorothy's, turned up and invited us all to a party. No. 1 Burlington Street, in Kemp Town, was a beautiful three-storey town house filled with period furniture and priceless antiques. It was owned by a titled gentleman euphemistically known as Adrian's 'Guardian'. The party was a surreal affair; everybody was pissed and apart from the cast and Dot's entourage, the rest of the guests were gay, even the dog who was a bitch was called George.

Bunny Lewis, our agent, an ex-military man, stiff upper lip and all that, didn't take it kindly when one of the gay guys made a play for him. He went berserk and a fight broke out. He pushed the gay guy into the glass cabinet, which housed a load of priceless Dresden china. It swayed precariously back and forth. Luckily I caught it just in time before it crashed to the floor. Dorothy was as usual centre of attention and taking no notice; she was on the sherry and being very loud. Emily happened to remark that she liked the lovely emerald green designer dress Dot was wearing so, without warning, Dorothy pulled if over her head and gave it to her. She spent the rest of the party in Adrian's dressing gown. Dorothy was always doing things like that; if you admired something she would just give it to you.

Dot loved a party, the trouble was, as soon as she'd had a few amontillados, she would pick a fight with someone and invariably one of the cast would get the sack. I don't know whether it was because she was high on adrenaline after the show or the demon drink, but she would pick on somebody and start insulting them for no apparent reason. I'd seen this scenario many times before; her eyes would narrow, the mouth would contort, reminiscent of the Sinatra lower lip twitch, and I knew somebody was going to get it. I didn't want it to be me so when the false eyelashes started to fall off I knew it was time to exit stage right. So making my excuses, I left. I decided to drive back to Bexley.

We were all staying with Dot that night: Bunny Lewis, Mike Housego, Kenny Brown and me. Emily, who was staying with her mother in Brighton, asked me if I could drop her off on the way. So, thinking my luck was in – I quite fancied the lovely Em in those days – we left the party. I dallied rather longer than I should have and when I got back to St Mary's Mount, Dorothy and her entourage had already arrived. Dot had gone to bed but the boys had waited up for me; they couldn't wait to tell me what had happened on the way home.

They were crying with laughter as they recounted the story. Dorothy had noticed that I wasn't in the car and asked where I was. Mike, not knowing who Emily was, unwittingly said I'd left with some bird with blond hair and big tits. Dorothy was pleased; she wasn't too crazy about my first wife ever since she'd thrown her out of our flat in Cardiff. Although I think Dorothy sitting on the toilet, with the door open, singing 'For Once in My Life' at the top of her voice at two o'clock in the morning and yelling 'it's gonna be a fucking smash', may have had something to do with it. Anyway, Dot was pleased I'd pulled a bird and asked who she was. 'I don't know,' said Mike, 'but she had a lovely mouth and great tits.' Dorothy, enjoying the story, asked what her name was. 'I dunno,' he said, 'Emily, something.' Making the connection, Dorothy hit the roof. 'That's my fucking niece,' she shrieked.

11

The Payola Scandal

It was Sunday 14 February 1971 when the shit hit the fan. We were all woken up that morning by Dorothy screaming blue murder. When I stumbled, bleary eyed into the kitchen, Dorothy was pacing up and down brandishing the *News of the World*. Splashed all over the front page was a picture of a bikini-clad Dorothy in Malta, posing with Jenny Howells, an independent song plugger. The headline screamed: 'Payola Scandal rocks the BBC.'

The article started reverberations throughout the BBC. A song plugger, who shall remain nameless for obvious reasons, had gone into Broadcasting House with a wire and recorded conversations incriminating many people in the music business and as someone said of the aforementioned song plugger: 'He sold his soul for two thousand quid.' Many people were dragged into the case. It was common knowledge at the time that record companies would employ record pluggers to get their records played on BBC Radio One and they would stop at nothing to get their records on the playlist. Producers were taken to dinner, disc jockeys were bribed with gifts and sexual favours; Janie Jones, a colourful flamboyant character, was arrested on suspicion of arranging parties at her home involving two-way mirrors and sex orgies for top BBC disc jockeys.

There are many parallels with Dorothy's life that resonate with today's events, the Jimmy Saville scandal being one of them. Dorothy had railroaded Emily into being a song plugger for her records. She asked her to wear a short skirt and go to see Jimmy Saville at his Radio Luxemburg office – big mistake – he asked Emily to sit on his lap whilst he was broadcasting, as he did with most young girls who he'd inveigled into his den. She did as she was asked for the sake of the plug but felt very uncomfortable about it. Later that night Emily met Dorothy for a meal at the Lotus House Chinese restaurant in Edgware Road. When they arrived Jimmy Saville was already at a table with a young girl. Emily, hanging back, told Dorothy she didn't want to stay because of Saville's unsavoury behaviour earlier. Dorothy, full of her usual Celtic charm, went over to him, cupped her hands over his ears, and warned him that if he touched her niece again she would cut his balls off and stuff them down his throat. Dorothy took no prisoners! Another parallel is the phone-hacking scandal; Dorothy was convinced that Murdoch had her house bugged. Mind you, she even thought that he'd put her on the CIA hit list in America. Who knows where truth began and paranoia took over with Dot. Emily remembers:

I hadn't seen Auntie Dorothy for some time and decided to call on her. She opened the door, looked furtively in both directions and whispered for me to come in. I thought nothing of it at the time; Dorothy often whispered when she had a show coming up, she said it saved her voice so I went along with it and spent the next quarter of an hour whispering. After a while I asked her where the concert was. 'There is no concert,' she whispered, 'the house has been bugged.' We all thought she was paranoid but who's to say, after the recent revelation, that she wasn't right; it was, after all Murdoch's Rag, the *News of the World*, that broke the Payola Scandal, naming Dorothy as the main protagonist.

Although there were a lot of people bribing DJs at the time there is no doubt in my mind that Dorothy was made the scapegoat. Song plugging was a cutthroat business in those days and some of the record companies could have been accused of sharp practice. It's been reported in the press that the big record companies would give records to shops in order to get their artists in the charts. Dorothy told me that:

Record companies were buying the records into the charts in those days. They would know which shops put the charts in and they would send people around these shops to buy the records. Once they got into the charts the BBC were honour bound to play them. I was in my agent's office and I saw boxes and boxes of records and when he was out of the room I had a look at the bloody records. And I'm damned, they'd bought this act – two brothers they were – into the charts. The sale of my recording of 'My Way' in Cardiff was so astronomical that I was accused of buying it in and they took me out of the charts. I was arrested for paying for my records to be played. If that was true I want my money back because they never bloody played them.

Things came to a head on 17 May that year. The way Dorothy described what happened next was as if she were describing a thriller movie:

I was driving home to Bexley from the West End, it was very late, there was virtually no traffic about and I happened to look in my rear-view mirror and saw a black car behind me. I don't know why but I was sure it was following me. I accelerated but the car followed, matching my speed but keeping its distance. I panicked and slammed my foot down and jumped some lights but the car was still on my tail. I screeched into my drive but the other car followed and two men jumped out. They asked me to get out of the car. I told them to fuck off, you won't rob me you bastards, I'll call the police. Then one of them said we *are* the police … CID. I said I don't believe you; you're some of Murdoch's thugs. Then one of the men tried to open the car door but I was too quick and locked it. He ran around the other side of the car and I tried to lock the passenger door too but I wasn't fast enough and the policeman dragged me out. I told them to take their fucking hands off me; they weren't going to pin a drink driving charge on me. I'll get my lawyers onto you I said; I thought this is great I couldn't pay for publicity like this. Then his mate said this is not about that and told me I was being arrested on suspicion of corruption and I wasn't obliged to say anything etc. etc. Then the bastards threw me into his car and took me to Bexley Police Station.

They told me to empty my pockets and take off any jewellery; they even made me take off my shoes; in case I harmed myself – it was bloody humiliating.

It sounds like a scenario from a situation comedy but this was no laughing matter; Dot was bound over to appear at Bow Street on charges of corruption. She was put in an excrement-daubed cell with Janie Jones, who'd been arrested on charges connected to the same BBC Payola case. It was alleged that Janie had arranged sex parties for disc jockeys in order to secure radio plays but Janie insisted that she had innocently held parties for President Records. It was also alleged that she ran an escort service for rich and titled clients but on this occasion it couldn't be proven. Dorothy started to bang on the bars of her cell yelling for them to let her out, 'I'm not a criminal, I'm a star,' she screamed. A butch looking policewoman yelled back, 'Keep it down Flossy'. Dorothy, incensed by this retort, shouted 'Who do you think you're calling Flossy, flat-foot … Are you married? No … I don't suppose you are,' she continued, 'who'd have you with fucking feet like that.' Dorothy remembers it as being the worst day of her life. This is her recollection of that traumatic event:

I was arrested at St Marys Mount Road, Bexley, Kent, on 17 May 1973. When I arrived at Bow Street Magistrates on the 20 July 1973, I was greeted by another onslaught of press, television and masses of well-wishers, who handed me flowers. I had to sign a paper on arrival and await bail. Two months had passed since I was arrested and taken to Bow Street Magistrates' Court. I had written about that horrific day in my ill-fated autobiography, *Rain, Rain Go Away*, events of which can never be erased. I'll never forget the time I arrived at the police station under the protection of eight police officers. A massive crowd had gathered – press and the public and yells of what have you done Dorothy? I recall shrugging my shoulders and shaking my head, I didn't even know what crime I'd committed to warrant such devilish diabolical treatment. I had to wait in the cell for other people; Janie Jones arrived in the police van. I shared the cell with thieves and dope addicts. That I did not mind, they were a happy bunch of people. I believe they'd arrived from Holloway Prison. I had little to no sleep, my mouth was parched … I was not even allowed a cup of tea; I was treated like the worst type of criminal. I recall seeing my handbag held upside down, the contents of which was searched. A demand from a police officer: 'Give me your glasses.' 'But I need them,' I said. 'Give them to me.' Then: 'Christ! how can you see through these?'

Then, two police officers, one on each of my arms, led me to the cell, which was approximately 6ft by 5ft. The walls were decorated with the previous victim's bowel waste, the stench fouled the airless cell. On the floor there was a urine-saturated mattress. There was another occupant. 'I'm Janie Jones,' she said; whom I'd heard of but never met. I came around some hours later soaked; I'd passed out, police had thrown water over me. At 5.30 p.m. that day Mr Edward Marks, chief clerk of my solicitors, M.A. Jacobs and Sons, had, I understand, been ordered to pay the bail before I was released. I understand that it was set at £500. Anyway, bail was set and 5.30 p.m. that day Mr Edward Marks, the chief clerk to my solicitors, paid the bail of £500 and I was allowed to go.

After suffering the indignity of being incarcerated overnight, she was released but it was to be three more years before the case came to court. Dorothy had to endure the worst three years of her life, wondering if she would be facing a custodial sentence. Her way of combating the stress, which almost resulted in her having a complete nervous breakdown, was by continuing to tour the country. Sometimes I think the only time she was happy was when she was on stage, lost in the adoration of her fans.

She'd loved and lost in her life but no one could take away the unquestionable love she felt from across the footlights. She was at home there but, when the curtain came down and she was alone in her grand mansion, her fragile mental state descended into total paranoia. She decided that she couldn't face living in the big house anymore; there were too many memories, good and bad. She'd been broken into at least five times, two of which were by inmates of the Bexley psychiatric hospital. One particular harrowing experience was when Dot found one of said inmates in her bedroom wearing one of her wigs. Seeing Dorothy, he panicked and made his escape through the window. It was no wonder she decided to convert the apple sheds adjoining the kitchen into an apartment. 'It will be my pad,' she said, 'I'll be safe from Murdoch there.' But that decision would almost cost her her life.

Building work started on the sheds adjoining the house with Dorothy overseeing things. The project seemed to have taken her mind off the impending doom of the trial and given her a new lease of life. Dorothy, mug of tea in hand, excitedly described her ideas about her new pad to David Pope, the builder who lived in the lodge. When the conversion work was finished Dorothy moved into her nest – her safe haven. This was more like it; her past problems were forgotten and for a while she was happy.

I spent many a pleasant hour with her in her American-style pad. It had an open-plan kitchen leading to the living area and a staircase leading to her bedroom, situated on an open mezzanine floor. Unthinkingly, I asked her why she wanted more living space; wasn't a twenty-two roomed house big enough? Dorothy lost it big time: 'I don't want to go into that fucking house anymore, don't you understand? It's been bad luck. Even Roger hated it. He wanted to pull it down and build a ranch-style bungalow in its place.'

Although Dot felt safe in her pad she still didn't go out much. She only ventured out when she had to work. I think she had become agoraphobic. She spent hours in bed, her beloved dog Jason by her side. Jason was an independent dog and often went missing for days on end but he always came back. On one particular occasion he was found wandering around Bexley Heath. The police brought him back and told Dot to take more care of him: 'He could get killed on the road one of these days.' But it wasn't a car that was to be the cause of Jason's tragic demise.

The impending trial was looming and Dorothy had been consulting a large legal book and scribbling furiously on legal pads into the early hours of the morning. When she decided she'd had enough, she went to bed, but she was awoken by the smell of burning in her nostrils. The wood panelled walls were going up like tinder. Not being able to see for the black evil smelling smoke, she groped for the open staircase that ran from her bedroom to the ground floor. In her panic she stumbled and fell down the whole length of the stairs. Stunned, she lay there, semi-conscious. The fire had spread from the main house. Rene, Dorothy's sister, who had been sleeping there at the time, raised the alarm. Soon there were firemen everywhere, fighting to save the beautiful mansion.

David Pope, hearing Dorothy's cry for help, kicked the door down, entered the blazing inferno and dragged the semi-conscious Dorothy to safety. Someone placed an oxygen mask on her face. As she started to come around she panicked and ripped off the mask and screamed: 'Where is he? Where is he? Jason … my lovely Jason.' Breaking free of the firemen, she ran towards the inferno in a desperate effort to save her beloved dog but before she got near the flames the firemen dragged her away kicking and screaming. She broke down sobbing uncontrollably, head in hands, muttering nonsense in her delirium about it all being Murdoch's fault.

Emily heard the news on the radio and rang Betty. She told her that Dorothy had been taken to Hilda's cottage in the village. The next morning Dorothy, still in her smoke-stained nightgown from the night before, was discussing with Hilda and Emily what would be the next best thing to do. Hilda suggested they try to find Jason; he might have got out somehow. Dorothy, still in shock from the previous night's trauma, couldn't face seeing the house she'd called home for thirty years in ruins. So Emily was elected to investigate.

The large Victorian mansion Emily had known and loved since childhood was now a smouldering shell. She picked her way gingerly through the blackened mess, everything was ruined; the solid silver Victorian champagne coolers had warped and melted in the heat and the once white grand piano, now blackened by smoke, was miraculously standing on legs that resembled burnt match sticks. It was the only thing recognisable in this once palatial pile. Emily gazed in silence at the devastation. Then, making her way towards the window, she stumbled on something; it was Jason, lying as if asleep behind a burnt-out sofa. There wasn't a mark on him; the acrid toxic smoke had asphyxiated him.

Emily, with tears welling up in her eyes, rushed into the garden. Through her tears she noticed something crawling on its belly across the lawn; it was Dorothy's terrified cat. Emily picked it up; it seemed that Harriet was the only survivor from that terrible night. On returning to Hilda's house Emily found Dorothy continuing to blame Murdoch for all her woes, insisting he was out to destroy her. Hilda, trying to appease her, told her to look on the bright side; she could have died in the fire. 'What bright side?' she sighed, 'The house was under insured and all I've got to look forward to, is being tried for corruption.' The house gradually deteriorated into a dilapidated state: the swimming pool, still full of water plus assorted garbage and debris, lay stagnant, giving rise to complaints from the neighbours about the danger that it was to inquisitive children. Eventually it was torn down. It's hard for me to believe that there are now twenty-two houses standing where the twenty-two-roomed mansion, with all its memories, once stood.

The Old Bailey

On 4 November 1974 Dorothy was brought before the Old Bailey charged with bribing Jack Dabbs, producer of *Four Way Family Favourites* to play her records, contrary to section (1) of the prevention of corruption act. Dorothy arrived accompanied by her secretary, Hilda. The co-accused, Jack Dabbs, arrived simultaneously in a separate car. A large crowd made up of Dot's fans and a few rubberneckers had assembled in front of the steps leading to the court. As Dot and Jack fought their way through the melee, the flock of felt-tipped assassins pounced, flash bulbs popping, and bombarded them with questions. I wasn't with her; Dorothy had asked me to be a witness for the defence. 'It will be good publicity for you,' she said. 'Get a new suit for the occasion.' Needless to say I declined; I didn't want to let her down but there was no way I was going to perjure myself in court.

In the Court Room

The court usher announced the case number '1283, the Crown versus Squires and Dabbs, Justice Neil McKinnon presiding'. Then the judge entered, took his seat and read out the charges:

Jack Dabbs of Saltdean, Brighton, you are charged that between JAN 1st and MAY 30th 1970 you corruptly agreed to accept from Dorothy Squires a gift or consideration payment of travel and hotel expenses incurred by you on a trip to Malta, as an inducement to play 'Eyes of the Beholder' a song, written by Dorothy Squires, on the programme, *World Wide Family Favourites*. How do you plead?

Jack pleaded not guilty then the judge read out the charges against Dorothy:

Mrs Dorothy Moore, also known as Dorothy Squires. You are accused of corruptly agreeing to give a gift or consideration of payment of travel and hotel expenses incurred by Jack Dabbs in visiting Malta and Gibraltar as an inducement or reward for playing 'My Way', sung by you, Dorothy Squires and 'Eyes of the Beholder' on the aforementioned programme. How do you plead?

Again the answer was not guilty then Stephen Mitchell, the prosecuting council, rose and called Dorothy to the stand. Dorothy took the oath and the cross-examination began. Stephen Mitchell asked Dorothy if it was a fact that that she had accompanied Mr Dabbs to Malta and Gibraltar in 1970 and wasn't it also a fact that she did pay Mr Dabbs' bill at the Sheraton Hotel in Valletta? Dorothy agreed that she had accompanied Jack to Malta and Gibraltar and that she had paid the hotel bill but insisted that she paid for the hotel in Malta because the Sheraton Hotel Valletta wouldn't take a cheque. 'Mr Dabbs was a friend of mine,' she continued, 'and I did what any friend would do; I paid for the bill in cash and Mr Dabbs refunded the money to me in cash when we returned to England.' Totally denying paying for anything for Jack Dabbs in Gibraltar, she explained that Jack was out there to cover the Song Festival and she was there to sing the new Gibraltar Anthem that had been written especially for her by Brian Willey. That was Dorothy's defence and nobody could prove otherwise. However, I knew the truth. When Dorothy had hissed into my ear on the night in question: 'The bastard is even putting his fags on the bill,' it was obvious to me that she was paying all Jack's expenses. Jack was a legend amongst song pluggers, notably because of his habit of going through the card whenever he was taken to lunch. On 7 November 1974 Dorothy was back at the Old Bailey to hear her fate. The judge, Mr Stephen Mitchell summing up, told the jury:

> It was alleged that Dorothy Squires paid for trips to Malta and Gibraltar in 1970 for radio producer Jack Dabbs, when he was in charge of *Four Way Family Favourites*. They were corrupt inducements or rewards for playing two records on the program. But it is only right that I should tell you the Crown's case is not a strong one, particularly as they relate to the charges concerning the visit to Gibraltar. According to Mr Jack Dabbs, Miss Squires did pay for the Malta trip, but as an innocent act of friendship; the Sheraton Hotel Valletta wouldn't take his cheque, so Miss Squires paid for it in cash and he refunded the money to Miss Squires, in cash when they returned to England.

The jury filed out to consider their verdict. When they returned they were asked if they had come to a unanimous decision. The foreman of the jury said they had and a piece of paper was handed to the judge. Dorothy and Jack nervously awaited the verdict. Judge Neil McKinnon read the note, pondered, then, removing his glasses, he announced to the court that they have been found not guilty. Dorothy broke down. Jack just stood impassively by her side. The judge continued: 'It is of the utmost public importance that corruption in all forms should be pursued and stamped out … but there should be no witch hunts. This case was not strong when it opened and it has not gained in strength since.'

Spontaneous applause broke out from the fans in the gallery and Dorothy broke down in floods of tears. On leaving the court, an ebullient Dorothy was mobbed by her fans. They'd brought bottles of champagne and the sparkling wine flowed onto the street. A reporter shoved a microphone under Dorothy's nose and asked her if she would like to make a statement. She said:

> Yes I bloody well would! I've been living with this nightmare for the last three years. I've been the victim of a witch-hunt by Murdoch. That bastard had to pick on me but I've been proved innocent. No one can stop me now; I'm going to finish my tour and hire the Palladium to give the biggest celebration concert anyone has ever seen.

With that, she spontaneously broke into a chorus of 'My Way' at the top of her voice. Although she had been found not guilty, the case had had a negative effect on her career; if she thought it was difficult getting plays before the trial, it was now to become almost impossible. The BBC wouldn't touch her. Even an appearance on *Ryan and Ronnie*, a TV show she'd recorded earlier for BBC Wales was pulled and Kenneth Griffith replaced her. Dorothy was convinced that she'd been put on a blacklist. Later the *Observer* exposed the fact that the BBC did indeed have a blacklist and published some of the names of people on it. Was Dorothy paranoid? ... I wonder! Dorothy did lose a lot of work because of the slur so, true to her word, she filed a case against Murdoch for defamation and loss of earnings. Dorothy often said that you do not win arguments by silencing those who have other views; you win them by stating your case forcefully and persuading people that you are right. She convinced herself that she was right and this case against Murdoch proved her convictions to be sound as the following transcript allegedly confirms:

CAUSE OF ACTION: order (15.R.2) (1) (2) (3) (4)

The First Defendant (Dorothy Squires) had been invited to the official opening of a newly built radio station of the B.F.B.S, 'The British Forces Broadcasting Service.' The said station was officially opened and broadcast by Mr Michael Aspel and the overlord of the festive occasion was the Governor General of the Island of Malta. The First Defendant had been accused in the *News of the World* and *The Sun* newspapers in a series of articles commencing on the 14 February

1971, of paying for a weekend flight to Malta, which left at midnight on the ensuing Monday. Cost of the Air Flight £43 3s 9d [Forty Three Pounds Three Shillings and Nine Pence] and purported to have been paid out of A.J. Music, a subsidiary company of Edward Kassner Associated Publishers Ltd of which the First Defendant held 49 per cent as testified by Mr David Dane, while being interrogated by Mr Mitchell at the Old Bailey.

Mr Dane knew this was not true as he was the accountant and Co-Director. The Second Defendant, (Mr Jack Dabbs'), air fare, according to David Dane, under oath, had been paid by A.J. Music Ltd, which leaves the obvious deduction: why wasn't the company A.J. Music's books, especially income tax books, produced at the trial at the Old Bailey, which would have proved that the First Defendant was not a Partner nor a Director of A.J. Music Ltd and did not pay for the Second Defendant's Air Flight or Hotel expenses, pursuant to which, Edward Kassner of President Records, Kassner Associated Publishers Ltd, David Dane, Accountant and Director, David Kassner (Son of Edward Kassner) Director, Victoria Haslam (Daughter of Edward Kassner) Brian M.D. Seed, secretary/director of Edward Kassner Associated Publishers Ltd and all of No. 11 Pine Street, London, EC1R, proving all are guilty of Perjury, Fraud, Conspiracy, Malicious Prosecution and Defamation , Re. A.J. Music Ltd, which resulted in the aforementioned trial.

Dorothy won her case and was awarded £30,000 in damages. I don't know how she got away with it; she *was* in fact a director of A.J. Music and owned 49 per cent of the shares. A contract stating this fact was signed on 12 January 1970 by David Dane (the accountant of Kassner Music) and Dorothy herself. Perhaps it was poetic justice that she didn't see a penny of the settlement. The vendetta against Murdoch showed no sign of abating and it wasn't long before Dorothy was back in court; this time to hear the verdict of a High Court libel action she'd taken out against The Murdoch Press and its show page writer, Weston Taylor, for an article he'd written called 'When Love Turned Sour'.

The article allegedly portrayed Dorothy as an 'embittered unprincipled woman willing to reveal details of her private life with Roger Moore for money.' The judge found in Dorothy's favour and she was awarded £4,400 damages. Following the verdict, Dorothy told the waiting paparazzi that she wasn't interested in the money only the verdict. 'What's the world coming to?' she said, 'The press shouldn't be allowed to get away with printing defamatory rubbish like this.'

Dorothy's appearances in court as a perpetual plaintiff, was about to be brought to an abrupt end. Her voracious litigiousness became so excessive that on 5 March 1987 she was banned from the High Court and declared to be a vexatious litigant. Vexatious litigants are individuals who persistently take legal action against others in cases without any merit and are forbidden from starting civil cases in courts without permission. This move against Dorothy by the courts was a rare thing – it was brought by the Attorney General Sir Michael Havers, who had himself been named, along with Director of Prosecutions and the Inland Revenue in her latest action. Opening the case, Council for the Attorney General told the court that 'Miss Squires has a voracious appetite for litigation'. There are a small group of people who persist in litigation and Dorothy was one of them. She would litigate over real and sometimes imagined grievances, regardless of cost and consequences. It's a psychiatric disorder, medically diagnosed as 'querulous paranoia' but she was never seen for formal psychiatric evaluation. Her litigation usually resulted from a slight or injustice, which assumed a special meaning for her and she used the courts to redress, what she believed to be an injustice. She was never able to accept any ruling against her. Her constant process of appeal against adverse decisions lasted many years and the cost for legal representatives and fees for writs and witnesses were enormous. Mr Justice Mann was told that Dorothy had started twenty court cases since 1982 and that nine had been dismissed as vexatious or frivolous. Amongst the multitude of actions she had brought there had been claims of defamation, assault, conspiracy and fraudulent misrepresentation against publishers, newspapers and solicitors 'I have no doubt,' he said, 'that she has habitually, persistently and without reasonable grounds initiated vexatious civil proceedings. These have resulted in High Court and Appeal Court actions and the Attorney General's application to have her declared a vexatious litigant should be allowed.' As the judge made his ruling Dorothy screamed, 'I'll fucking sue *you*, you bastard; this is not the end – it is only the beginning. I am going to get my fans in their thousands to march down Whitehall!' Then, appearing on the steps of the High Court, furious and in full voice, she yelled, 'They've gagged me.'

She announced to the fans and press who were gathered outside: 'It's a bloody joke to say I have a voracious appetite for litigation. I don't want to be a bloody litigant, I just want to be a singer. That's my job. I want to get on with my career.' A reporter, pushing a microphone toward her, asked if she was going to appeal. 'You bet your sweet life I'm going to appeal,' she said. 'I'll go to the House of Lords. I will even take it to the European Court of Justice if necessary.' And so litigation curtailed, for the time being at any rate, Dorothy resumed her tour of the country. The adage that no publicity is bad publicity was borne out by the fact that all the shows were sell-outs – except Cardiff.

It was an Easter Sunday and the Capitol Cinema, a 2,000-seat auditorium, in the centre of Cardiff, was only half full. Dorothy was furious: 'Is this all the thanks I get when I come back to my own country? They don't fucking support me?' Bunny Lewis, trying to appease her, explained that Easter Sunday was a bad day to stage a concert. 'People are on holiday,' he said. Dorothy was having none of it and stormed out. In the dressing room I could hear Dorothy's entrance music strike up but something was wrong; Dorothy wasn't singing. I went to the side of the stage to investigate, only to find Dorothy berating the audience in no uncertain terms: 'We've sold out every major theatre in the country,' she yelled, 'but when I come back home to Wales you don't support me.' Then picking on Shirley Bassey's mother, who happened to be in the front row, she continued, 'And Shirley won't come back either, ask her mother. And another thing, they had to cancel a Harry Seccombe concert because of poor bookings. It seems the Welsh don't support their own.' I thought the audience would walk out; the people she was berating were the very the fans who had bothered to support her. After this tirade, she sailed into 'Say It With Flowers' as if nothing had happened and, amazingly, she got another standing ovation.

After the show we all went for a meal. Dot was in a foul mood. Bunny Lewis, who had been press-ganged by Dot into operating the follow spot all night, was knackered. He was supposed to drive Dorothy back to London but he got so plastered on champagne after the show that his elbow slipped off the restaurant table and he fell on the floor. This was the last straw. 'You had no right to get pissed,' she yelled. 'The last thing I want to do after singing my fucking guts out for two hours is to drive myself back to London.' Still seething, and with Bunny slumped in the passenger seat, she covered the 150 miles in 2 hours flat.

The next stop was the ABC Hull. The show had gone really well and afterwards the boys of the band had gone out on the town. I went to a nightclub to see the Ballet Montparnasse, a dance troupe I'd worked with in the *Lonnie Donegan Show* some years earlier. When I got back to the Railway Hotel, Nicky Welch, Mike Housego and Kenny Brown were sitting in the foyer drinking and recounting their sexual exploits. Nicky was unconscious. There was no two ways with Nicky, he never seemed to get drunk; he was either awake or unconscious. When Kenny got to a particularly juicy story about some girl he'd pulled. Nicky stirred from his drunken stupor and mumbled, 'Shut up you'll give me the fucking horn', then promptly fell back to sleep.

We were about to retire when the first violinist ran into the hotel demanding to see Nicky. Nicky, coming out of his comatose state, demanded to know what all the yelling was about. The violinist was fit to burst a blood vessel. He told us that the boys of the band had been watching porn on TV and the guitar player had got a little carried away and tried to get his leg over the landlady's 15-year-old daughter. The cops had been called and the said guitarist was banged up in the local nick. Nicky warned us all not to tell Dorothy; she'd had enough bad publicity to last a lifetime. The last thing she needed was another scandal. He would sort it out in the morning. We were due to do the next concert in Halifax. Nicky, thinking we would be a man down, booked another guitar player from the BBC's Northern Dance Orchestra. Fortunately, our original guitar player was let off with a caution. Unfortunately, Nicky couldn't cancel the guitar player from the NDO, so we ended up with the two of them on the stage at the same time. Nicky naively thought that Dot wouldn't notice the extra musician amongst the twenty-five strong orchestra but when she turned to acknowledge the band she spotted him. I don't know how Nicky explained it but nothing more was said and another crisis was averted.

The tour was a resounding success, finishing a year to the day back at the Palladium. Dorothy was back in the public eye now and in demand as a cabaret artist: earning £7,000 a week, a huge amount even by today's standards and this was the seventies. The UK had the biggest nightclub scene in the world at the time; most towns had at least one. Clubs like the Batley Variety Club, Allison's Theatre Club in Liverpool, The Talk of the North Manchester and the Wakefield Theatre club attracted international artists from all over the world: Louis Armstrong, Gene Pitney, Sammy Davies Jnr, Shirley Bassey, Tom Jones and Dorothy was one of them too.

Dorothy was appearing at the Double Diamond Club in Caerphilly, one of the biggest clubs in Wales, when she received word from her agent that she had been booked to top the bill at London's Talk of the Town. She was ecstatic. The last time she'd played it was when she'd walked out after the acrimonious altercation with the management over her billing and she never thought that she would ever be asked back. Nobody walked out on the Grade Organisation; Lew and Leslie Grade along with their brother Bernard Delfont were the most powerful people in British show business at the time. So, to be asked back to top the bill was, in Dot's eyes, a particularly sweet victory.

Her opening night was a happening to rival her Palladium concert in 1970. She'd augmented Burt Rhodes' already large orchestra with six violins, four violas and two cellos; the orchestra stretched from one side of the stage to the other. Dorothy did nothing by halves; all the stars had turned out to see her and she wasn't about to fail in front of her peers. The aftershow party in her dressing room was the usual sycophantic soirée with Dorothy centre stage accepting the plaudits of the crowd. The fawning flatterers had been joined by the stars that'd turned out to see her: Shirley Bassey, with her then husband Sergio, Vince Hill and his wife Annie, Kenny Brown and girlfriend Lita Rosa and skiffle king Lonnie Donegan.

Dorothy was on a terrific high; the combination of adrenaline from her triumph, Purple Hearts and flowing champagne was a potent mix and Dorothy was being a little more self-opinionated than usual. The eyelashes had started to peel off and things had started to turn ugly. When Dorothy had had a few drinks she changed like Jekyll and Hyde and would goad someone until it would inevitably end in a blazing row. Turning to Shirley Bassey's husband, Dorothy told him that he'd better look after her because she was a good woman. This spark ignited an already inflammable situation between the other Welsh diva and her second husband, Sergio, and war broke out. Lita Rosa, rising to the feminist bait, accused Kenny of drinking too much and threatened to grass him up to the police about his drug habit. Kenny protested that Lita was saying this out of spite because she knew it was all over between them; he had never taken drugs in his life. Then, she pushed him down the stairs. Visualising mayhem, Bunny Lewis said, 'Come on John, this is where we came in,' and we beat a hasty retreat: Bunny to his house in Chaney Walk and me to Dorothy's house in Bray to await the diva's return.

12

The House at Bray

When St Mary's Mount had been reduced to a smouldering ruin, Dorothy had gone in search of somewhere else to live. She knew Roger was living in Denham Village and she wanted to live nearby. For all her protestations that Roger was history, she was still obsessed with him. She'd heard that Larry Forrester, the author of the Oscar-nominated film *Tora! Tora! Tora!* was leaving the country for tax reasons and was looking for a quick sale for his house at Bray. Dorothy, knowing Denham Village to be less than 30 miles from Bray, made Larry an offer he couldn't refuse – she got it for £42,000 cash. This was a lot of money in the seventies but a steal when you think that Langtry House was purported to have been built for Lilly Langtry by her lover the Prince of Wales, who later became King Edward VII. The next time it went for sale it fetched £1.5 million.

The grand house in the Fisheries at Bray had been split into three parts: North Wing, The Minstrels and South Wing Bray Lodge, the North Wing being Dorothy's new pile while Sheila Ferguson of the Three Degrees resided in the South Wing. It was a beautiful house, which shared its lovely location on the Thames with a host of famous and dare I say it infamous people, all of whom had houses nearby. The lodge next door was owned by an old colonel type who wanted to sell. Dorothy contacted her old friend Billy Smart, the circus owner, who was very interested in buying in the area and set up a meeting at her house. Billy offered to buy the house for ready cash. The old gent, being old school, wouldn't accept cash. Dorothy, who had arranged the meeting, became very abusive towards the poor old fellow and threw him out.

Dorothy's part of the house needed decorating and refurbishing from top to bottom so Des Brown, a long-time fan of Dorothy's came to the rescue. Des had been running his own building business and could do anything – electrics, plumbing, carpentry – you name it. And so, Des moved into the North Wing with his partner Peter Bennett and started the renovations. It took over a year to complete. I say complete, nothing was ever complete with Dorothy; she was always adding another room or wing, the most impressive being the River Room, which as the name suggests looked onto the Thames. The property also boasted a private mooring but Dorothy, not owning a boat, didn't have much use for it so she rented it to a financial adviser called Barry. Barry had been renting a few doors away and was given notice to leave. So Dorothy, always a sucker for a sob story, said he could moor his boat at her place and if he wanted to he could move into the spare room.

As you entered North Wing from Fisheries Road, you were faced with a split-level ground floor. On the higher level was the dining room, the lower level being the lounge. To the right of the lounge was the television room that had French windows that opened onto a beautiful lawn that swept past the Dutch elm tree down to the private mooring at the bottom of the garden. Upstairs there were seven bedrooms with the master having an en suite. The free-standing Jack and Jill bathroom at the top of the stairs was reminiscent of a Dickensian tuck shop with its bow windows glazed with bottle glass.

None of the contents of St Mary's Mount had been insured but Dorothy managed to salvage some of her priceless furniture, which now stood in pride of place in her new home. The refractory table and some of her monk furniture graced the new dining room, and the French wardrobe, purported to be one of only two made, the other being bought by Grace Kelly, took pride of place in Dot's bedroom – although she had to cut a hole in the ceiling to accommodate the grand piece. The stained-glass window that was set in the front door of Bexley was now set into the ceiling at Bray and used as an impressive down light.

This magnificent pile became my new digs when I stayed with Dot when working in the area. It wasn't Bexley of course, with its wild showbiz parties and all its memories, it had a different vibe; it was more intimate, more of a home. She still had lots of visitors though; she was surrounded by stars. Across the road were Laurie Holloway and his lovely wife Marion Montgomery, Michael Parkinson lived on the corner and just down the Fisheries were Terry Wogan and Rolf Harris. The Roux brothers' Thames-side restaurant was just down river as well. But all the aforementioned celebs paled into insignificance by one guest that dropped in.

Allan Jones, the forties Broadway and film star arrived at Dorothy's in 1976. Allan, whose family hailed from Merthyr Tydfil, had topped the charts in America with 'The Donkey Serenade' – long before his son Jack inherited his fine tenor voice and had hits of his own. Making his grand entrance by boat, this large handsome man with an enormous personality to match, strode ashore, his silver mane blowing in the wind, reminiscent of a conquering hero arriving in a movie. Dot, ignoring the young starlet he had on his arm, quipped, 'Where have been you Welsh bastard, you're late for dinner.'

During that summer, I was booked to do a week's cabaret at Jenkinson's Cabaret Bar in Brighton. As Dorothy's house was only an hour away, I decided to commute. When I arrived, I was greeted by Dorothy with her usual Welsh hospitality: 'I suppose you're hungry,' then turning to Mary, the Welsh maid, she said, 'go make this prick some chips.' Mary, who was very religious, stammered, 'Here's a house to be a Mormon in isn't it,' and retired tout suite to the kitchen.

Emily had moved in with Dorothy at this time because she felt that Dot needed someone to be with her after all the traumas she'd endured. I had always been attracted to the lovely Em, ever since that night in Brighton and I asked her if she would like to go with me to the gig. Dot, ever the matchmaker said, 'Go on Em, go with him, he's lonely.' When we got back that night Dorothy was still up. Not renowned for her sensitivity, she was about as subtle as a rubber cosh, she said, 'Right, am I making one bed up, or are you two buggers going to be crawling across the landing all night?' Emily was a lovely girl and with me being estranged from my first wife, the inevitable happened. When I awoke the next morning, Dorothy, Emily and Hilda were already in the kitchen having breakfast. When I appeared, Dorothy turned to Hilda and remarked, 'What do you think of these two buggers doing a double act?' I'll never forget the time I spent at that lovely house, not least that beautiful summer or the bedroom I shared with Emily, where the sun glinted off the water of the Thames, casting crepuscular rays onto its butterscotch walls.

The next time I stayed at Bray was when I was booked to sing on the Miss Wales contest, which was being recorded for the BBC. Brian Turvey, a BBC producer, was making a documentary about Dorothy and had been filming that day. After the shoot, my wife Olwen and I and Brian and his wife were invited to dinner. Dorothy as usual was in charge of the cooking, assisted by Emily. We all sat down to what we thought was going to be a pleasant evening meal when Dorothy, who after imbibing on the ubiquitous sherry, started to insult Emily. Here we go again I thought; she could never resist the little digs, the sophomoric cheap shots, like picking at a scab. She would start by trying to goad someone, looking for their Achilles heel. She did it to me once by having a go at my Dad. But she would only do this when she had an audience. Emily was well used to this and would invariably just shrug it off. She knew that it would all be forgotten when Dot was sober. But this particular night Dorothy went too far. She started by insinuating that Emily only liked married men, knowing full well that Em and I had had a dalliance. It's hard to know why she did this, as it was she who'd instigated the affair in the first place. Anyway, if she thought that she would cause trouble between my wife Olwen and me, she had another thing coming. I had no secrets from Olwen; she knew all about my amorous assignation with Emily.

Olwen kicked me under the table and whispered to me in Welsh, 'Cymra dim sylw, John', which roughly translated means 'Take no notice'. Little did we know at the time that Dorothy understood what she'd said. I'd never heard

Dorothy speak Welsh, except for the odd idiom but having been brought up in a predominantly Welsh area she understood every word. She kept goading Emily until at last Emily snapped and told Dorothy a few home truths about her own infidelities with married men. Dorothy screamed at Emily not to talk to her like that and full-scale war broke out, resulting in her storming off. There were two sets of stairs in the house, one that led from the dining room to the upstairs landing, and another that led from the kitchen at the other end of the house. Dorothy stomped up the stairs that led from the dining room and we could hear her footsteps thumping overhead until she reached the other set of stairs, which led from the kitchen. She stomped down them and burst back into the room, screaming, 'And another thing you're too fucking fat.' Emily retaliated with, 'I may be fat but I can go on a diet but you're an old lady.' Dorothy completely lost it and screamed, 'I'm not an old lady I'm a star,' and smacked Emily across the face. Brian and his wife stared open mouthed at this tirade; they hadn't seen this side of Dorothy before. They were due to stay the night but tactfully made their excuses, saying that he had to be back in Cardiff for a meeting. In the morning, Dorothy arrived at breakfast as if nothing had happened, and invited us to go racing with her at Newbury. We diplomatically declined and left for Cardiff and Dorothy and Emily left for the races. Her extravagant hobby was costing her a lot of money so, in order to fund it, she took a contract to appear at the South Sydney Juniors' Club in Australia. Dorothy hated to travel alone so she cashed in her first-class airfare for two club-class tickets, and she and Emily flew on Pan Am to Sydney.

13

Australia

The club scene in Sydney in the seventies was booming. They were amazing places that catered for the whole family. The South Sydney Juniors, for instance, had a cabaret room that held about 500 people, a ballroom, restaurant, indoor swimming pool and a gambling room that housed about a hundred 'One Arm Bandits' or 'Pokey Machines' as the Aussies call them. The host of international stars that appeared there were backed by Lionel Huntingdon and his fifteen-piece orchestra and *this* was just a rugby club! Emily remembers:

> Auntie Dorothy always toured her own musical director and drummer and one night Dorothy's pianist got so pissed that when he tried to count the band in with a-one, a-two, a-one two three, he fell arse over tit into the orchestra pit and Pip the drummer had to take over as musical director for the rest of the night.

Ever the professional, Dorothy finished her show and made her exit. Emily was waiting to help her out of her stage clothes when Dot burst into her dressing room. 'I'll fucking kill him,' she screamed. Emily, trying to calm her down said: 'You can't go on like this Auntie Dorothy, effing and blinding all over the place.' Dorothy, ignoring this advice, continued her rant and made for the door. Terrified of what she might do, Emily locked the door and stuffed the key down her cleavage. 'I'll give it back to you when you calm down,' she said. Dorothy, advancing menacingly towards her yelled, 'You don't think that's going to fucking stop me do you?' Eventually she calmed down and Emily let her out. Thankfully she didn't hit the pianist but she gave him a right old roasting.

To say Dorothy wasn't very happy in Australia would be an understatement; the audience was hostile towards her. The thing with Australians is they're a great audience if they like you, but if they take a dislike to you, look out. They even gave Frank Sinatra a hard time and he left promising never to return. If they disliked Sinatra's attitude, they disliked winging 'Poms' more and Dorothy's act was filled with depressing reminiscences about her break up with Roger. She wasn't doing the business either. It didn't help that the door staff were telling people that her show wasn't very good. She had been contracted for six weeks but she was asked to leave after just three, although they would pay her for the whole six weeks. Dorothy was adamant; she'd never reneged on a gig in her life and she wasn't about to start now. Luckily, the business started to pick up and she was allowed to fulfil her contract.

Whilst she was in Oz, the publisher Robin McGibbon flew in to try to persuade her to write her autobiography. Dorothy told him the only one that could write *her* biography was Harold Robbins because her life story read like a novel. Harold Robbins was contacted by McGibbon and Dorothy received a telegram from Robbins saying, because of his commitments he wouldn't be able to undertake it until 1977. So Dorothy decided to write the book herself.

14

Dorothy's Book

Everyone thought that McGibbon must have been crazy to agree to let Dorothy write the book herself, but his faith in her ability was justified when she managed to write what was little short of an epic. It was a fascinating story but the book was doomed from the start.

Dorothy hadn't signed the contract and was proving to be very difficult to pin down. McGibbon went to Dorothy's house to try to get her to sign. It was a genial evening with Dorothy cooking hamburgers and pouring fine wine. The niceties over, Robin wanted to know where he stood. He'd made Dorothy, in my opinion, a very fine offer and was in no mood to haggle. There were two options on the table, both excellent for Dorothy. One option was to sell the serialisation rights, without which Robin wasn't prepared to continue. Dorothy had already received a £10,000 advance without serialisation and there was no way Robin could get his money back. The other option was Everest Books were prepared to pay £5,000 on signature of contract, £12,000 on receipt of manuscript and £3,000 on publication and of course a 75 per cent cut of any sales over the first £20,000. He was bending over backwards in an effort to seal the deal and offered 90 per cent over the first £30,000.

After this meeting, Dorothy fell out with Robin McGibbon big time. She claimed that she never gave her permission for him to serialise her story in the *Sunday People* newspaper and took out an injunction preventing its publication. Their relationship went from bad to worse. She told a well-known journalist that she would 'do anything to nail that bastard.' She also made unfounded allegations about him to BBC presenter Pete Murray before going on air, claiming that McGibbon had done two years' jail for business deception. McGibbon took her to court and sued her for slander. His defence told the court that the background to this was a dispute about the decision of his client to publish the book and in no way were these slanderous remarks true. She counterclaimed that the letter McGibbon wrote to Harold Robins was defamatory because it drew attention to her involvement in the Payola Case. The judge found for Mr McGibbon and Dorothy was ordered to pay £10,000 damages and costs.

The biggest problem preventing publication, however, wasn't her disputes with McGibbon. Dorothy didn't take into account the fact that you have to be careful not to libel anyone. After reading the final proofs Goodman, Derrick & Co., the lawyers for the publisher, sent her a letter pointing out many defamatory passages. Dorothy was slagging off everybody. Having lived with Roger in Hollywood for seven years, she'd picked up all kinds of gossip about the stars of the day and didn't bother to check their authenticity. She libelled Anthony Newly by describing in detail his sexual predilections; alleging that he used to make one of his four wives dress up in school uniform for his sexual gratification. I'm not sure which wife she meant and with Anthony not around to defend himself, I don't suppose we'll ever know if it was true or not. She libelled Edmond Purdom, the star of the film *The Student Prince*, claiming that he had photographed one of his four wives whilst she was in bed with her boyfriend. She libelled Billy Reid for making her have a number of illegal abortions. She libelled the doctor who was alleged to have prescribed the wrong medication for her mother, resulting in her death. She libelled Robert Nesbitt, the famous producer, by accusing him of being an 'arrogant lord of creation' because he had to have his name bigger on the bill than the stars. She even had a go at one of her contemporaries Vera Lynn and she accused Nat Jackly's wife of making him a nervous wreck.

One of her biggest mistakes though was maligning Lew and Leslie Grade, her former agents. She described them as the cloven-hoofed gentlemen, which was tantamount to committing professional suicide. Between them the Grades and their brother Bernard Delfont ran show business in Britain. Lew Grade was the head of ATV and Bernard Delfont ran half the theatres in the West End. He was also involved in the film industry and was instrumental in bringing the Royal Variety performance to television. She accused them of being a monopoly that was strangling the business. And last but not least she accused Rupert Murdoch of being the cause of her downfall. In retrospect, who would say Dorothy wasn't right in her accusations; a family that ran television, film and theatre would certainly not be allowed today by the monopolies commission, and as far as Murdoch is concerned enough said.

Some of this vitriol was probably true but unless it's in the public domain and can be proven, or the people are dead, you can be in real trouble. However, most of the people she'd maligned are dead by now and so, were it to be published today, she might well get away with it. I'm sure it would make fascinating reading if it was to surface but the proofs have vanished from sight. To this day no one knows what happened to them.

According to Stoy Hayward, the chartered accountants that oversaw Dorothy's bankruptcy, the manuscripts, galley proofs and Roger Moore's private letters to Dorothy were seized by bailiffs and thrown into a pantechnicon along with her furniture and taken to Reading but Dorothy was convinced that Robin McGibbon still had them. This is a letter she wrote after they parted company:

197 Trebanog Road
Trebanog Porth
Mid Glamorgan
CF39 9JU

April 8, 1997
Robert David McGibbon Esq.
27 Burford Roas, Bickley, Kent BRI 2EY

Dear Robin McGibbon,

I write with reference to the agreement of 2 January 1976, between myself and your former company, Everest Books Limited, entered into for the purpose of publishing 'with reasonable promptitude' an autobiography written entirely by myself under the title, Rain, Rain, Go Away. I duly delivered the typescript of this book to you and your company, and in January 1977 you printed galley proofs of the said work. In May 1977, I delivered to you and your company an additional 20,000 words approved by Counsel, Mr Patrick Milmo, to replace passages in the typescript that were the subject of objections raised by Roger and Luisa Moore. As you are aware, the copyright of the typescript, the galley proofs, and the additional 20,000 words, belongs entirely to me. In case any doubt on this subject should remain, I hereby assert my right to be identified as the author of Rain, Rain, Go Away, in accordance with the Copyright, Designs and Patents Act 1988. In the event of my death, the typescript, the galley proofs, the additional 20,000 words, and the copyright thereof, will become assets of my estate, to be controlled by a literary executor nominated by myself. Although my book is neither your property nor your copyright, you have retained the typescript, the galley proofs and the additional 20,000 words. On 5 August

1994, you allowed Jessica Davies, a journalist then employed by the Daily Mail, to come to your home and to read parts of my unpublished book. She quoted directly from its contents in her article, 'The Star Who Loved and Lost,' published in the Daily Mail on 6 August 1994. In return for allowing Jessica Davies access to my work you received from Associated Newspapers the sum of £1,200. As a professional writer and former publisher, you do not need to be told that your action in this respect was illegal and in gross breach of copyright. My rights in that matter are reserved, but I am prepared to waive them in exchange for your agreement to return to me the typescript, the galley proofs, and the additional 20,000 words of Rain, Rain, Go Away; accompanied by an undertaking that you will never again seek to benefit from this material either during my lifetime or after my death.

Yours faithfully,
Dorothy Squires

Robin McGibbon claimed that the book debacle was the cause of the downfall of his company and on 17 July 1981 he decided to go into voluntary liquidation. A meeting was held at a London Hotel. Dorothy, accompanied by her secretary Hilda, arrived late for the meeting. Bursting into the conference room, she sneered, 'Is this the McGibbon fiasco?' McGibbon sat motionless with his fiancée, the actress Sue Tompsett. The liquidator, Mr Solomon Lipmann, told the creditors that one of the major reasons for Everest Books' downfall was the failure to publish Miss Squire's book Rain, Rain, Go Away. Continuing, he said that the company, founded in 1973, was delighted when it received the rights to publish the autobiography because it hoped the book would improve its ailing financial circumstances but, unfortunately, Everest Books was restrained from publishing Miss Squires book by a High Court order.

The five-year dealings between Dorothy and McGibbon had been dogged with legal problems; Roger Moore had taken out a High Court order preventing publication of love letters he had written to Dorothy, then to cap it all, Dorothy also took out an injunction restraining publication. When she was asked why she had taken out a court order, she refused to give her reasons. Robin McGibbon said the company has spent £40,000 producing the book already, which it was then unable to publish. Dorothy, however, swore she would not be dropping the order, which she was bringing against the company for breach of contract. The meeting finished with Dorothy and McGibbon coming face to face in the foyer of the hotel. An argument broke out and Dorothy boasted to McGibbon that she had ten publishers interested in bringing out her book, which she was rewriting and updating. McGibbon challenged her publicly to name them. But she refused, simply saying: 'Who would not want to publish it!'

15

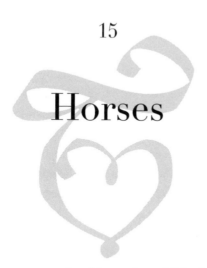

Horses

After her failed attempt to get her biography published, Dorothy went on a blinkered quest to win the Grand National. Dorothy had loved horses ever since the days when, as a kid, she rode Dolly, the family pony. But when Bunny Lewis, her agent, suggested to Dot that she should buy a half share in a racehorse, she was a bit reticent. She joked that if she were to buy a half share she wanted the front half because that's the part that passes the winning post first. 'But with my luck,' she quipped, 'the bastard will come in backwards.' Bunny reasoned, that being part of the racing fraternity would bring her publicity that could further her career, but Bunny had not banked on Dorothy's obsessive nature; she wasn't content to be a part owner of anything. She started buying race horses as if they were going out of style ending up owning six: Walburswick, Knockaulin, Fair Gazette, Norwegian Flag, Dewi Sant and Esban.

Esban was by far the best horse she ever bought. Dorothy went to the Dublin horse auctions to bid for him. He was the most expensive but she had the bit between her teeth now, if you'll excuse the pun, and was determined to get him. With her predilection for litigation, buying racehorses trained by

Bob Clay and Jenny Pitman – and they didn't come cheap – it was no wonder that her extravagancies ultimately lead to her financial downfall. She tried to get the cost of her horses offset against her tax, claiming they were a great way of promoting her career. She almost won her case too but she fell at the last hurdle and they were disallowed. Dorothy remembers:

I went over to Ireland with Bob Clay, I'd never met him before he came to St Mary's Mount and we went over to Goff's Sale, *the* leading bloodstock auctioneer in Ireland. I decided I wasn't going to pay more than £500 for a horse. On the plane going over Bob said there's a horse there that I'd probably get for two grand. I said I'm not paying £2,000 for a horse you must be joking. He said wait till you get there. It was Esban he was talking about. He didn't come in to the sale ring until the afternoon. I'd been to see him in his box and I said to Bob Clay, you'll never get him for two grand. When he came into the ring I'd never seen anything so beautiful in all my life; he was like a rocking horse; he was a special grey; you'd think he'd been painted he was so beautiful. And he had red socks on. If Bob thought we would get him for two thousand he was dreaming.

I was up against stiff opposition from the guys in their camel hair coats. The bidding opened up at £5,000. And he was withdrawn at nine and a half thousand guineas. I went to leave and Bob said where you going I said I'm going to buy that horse are you coming? There was a bunch of the guys in camel hair coats haggling and Paddy Murphy, the trainer; he was telling them that he wasn't for sale. I waited for them to go and I said I'll give you £10,000 for him. He said give me £10,250 and he's yours – I knew he was sticking the £250 on top for himself so I said no, I'll give you ten thousand and that's it. What I didn't know at the time was that Esban's owner was a woman, Mrs Ashmore, and she wanted him to go to another woman and I got him for ten grand. I called Hilda, my secretary and I said Hilda I've bought a horse. I said I paid ten thousand for it. There was a pause at the other end. I said are you there she said hang on a minute I'm on the floor I've just dropped the phone. She said you must be bloody mad.

Esban was running the next day in Leopards town in Dún Laoghaire against Sea Brief who was owned by Arkle's owner; the Duchess of Westminster and I remember praying to my Dad, I said please Dad if you've got any influence with the man upstairs keep him safe for me. I went to see him run at Leopards town and it was a photo finish between three of them. He went on to win the Scottish National and come a second in the Welsh National at Chepstow.

After the race Paddy Murphy made me promise that I would never run him in the Grand National. On the other hand Norwegian Flag, the next horse I bought, was out of the same Dam; they were brothers but he was a natural Aintree Horse. I had six in the end the last one was born on St David's day and I called him Dewi Sant; that's Welsh for St David.

Dorothy inherited her love of horse racing from her father, the travelling showman, and at one time he'd owned a champion trotter. She always joked that, 'Dada had given all his money to sick animals, but he didn't know they were sick when he backed them.' Archie was a hell of a gambler and I'm sure he would have been proud to have been around in the days when his daughter was a top racehorse owner. Emily remembers when, as a child, she would spend the weekends at Dorothy's, Archie could always be found ensconced with his cronies in the smoke-filled library at St Mary's Mount, watching the racing. The house rang to the yells of 'Come on my son', when they were winning and 'Iesu Grist' (Jesus Christ in Welsh) when they would lose. Emily remembers not liking Archie very much because he smelt of smoke but Archie obviously loved her. After the race he would take off his omnipresent peaked cap, or Dai cap as we say in Wales, and pass it amongst his pals for them to toss in all their loose change, which he would then give to young Emily as pocket money to take back to the convent.

Dorothy had some real success at the races. In 1973 her horses Esban and Norwegian Flag placed her amongst the leading National Hunt owners, just one place behind the Queen Mother. She was often seen in the Royal enclosure, but as the old adage goes 'you can take the girl out of the valleys but you can't take the valleys out of the girl.' She could be very loud and embarrassing; when Esban, her best horse managed to win the Crudwell Cup at Warwick in March 1976, the ever dramatic Dot went wild, kissing everyone in sight, starting with her horse, her jockey and anyone else within kissing range. After Esban's success in winning the Scottish National, Dorothy had eyes on the ultimate prize.

She always said that she would never run a horse in the Grand National because it was too dangerous but she changed her mind after seeing Norwegian Flag take the Queen Mother's horse, Inch Arran, to a photo finish at Aintree. 'He took to the course like duck to water,' she said. 'He flew over the fences like a bird.' This convinced her that the Flag could win the National and entered him in the 1974 event. Dorothy was appearing in Cabaret at the 'Stardust Club' in Usk in the run-up to the race but she was determined to be hands on with The Flag's preparation. She commuted to Wolverhampton every day to watch Bob Clay training Norwegian Flag for what she hoped would be the jewel in the crown of her racing career.

Dot was brimming with confidence; he was the second favourite, two years younger than Red Rum and two stone lighter. Before any race, Dorothy would always go into the enclosure and whisper encouragement in the horse's ear, in Welsh. She swore blind the horses understood her Celtic murmurings and recognised her when they sniffed the Joy perfume that she always wore: 'I went into his box; he always shivered when he was being saddled up and I whispered up his nose to calm him down. I'm sure he knew me by my perfume.'

Norwegian Flag didn't win the Grand National that day; it was won by Red Rum but he did well enough to give Dorothy hope that he would win the National one day, but it wasn't to be. In March 1977 Dorothy was at Sandown to see Norwegian Flag run for the last time. He was going like a train when tragedy struck; he was brought down by Castle Gay. Dorothy jumped to her feet in panic and ran to the rails, praying that he hadn't been hurt. But the Flag was critically injured; he'd broken his back and would have to be put down. Dorothy was inconsolable. 'Don't let them put a bullet in his head,' she screamed.

Whilst being interviewed after the tragedy, she broke down. 'My Lovely Flag,' she sobbed, 'Why is everything I love taken from me? I lost my husband to an Italian actress, my lovely home in Bexley was burned to the ground, I even lost my dog in the blaze and now Norwegian Flag.' Such was her paranoia and hatred of Murdoch, whom she blamed for all her ills, that she convinced herself that the horse's death was part of a vendetta against her by the infamous newspaper baron. Dorothy vowed that he'd never stop her. 'Racing is a great leveller,' she said. 'There are no knives in your back on the racecourse; we are all the same on the turf or under it – we are all equal.'

Through her connection with the sport of kings she rubbed shoulders with a number of the Royal family but it wasn't her only connection with aristocracy. Her friendship with Barbara Cartland was forged through a meeting with Dorothy's old friend and producer, Norman Newell. Dame Barbara had decided to make an album of love songs with the Royal Philharmonic Orchestra, which was produced by Norman and Dorothy was invited to the session. Dame Barbara recalled:

I'd heard vaguely of her turbulent quarrels, her unhappiness when Roger Moore left her, her numerous court cases and many other things including her enormous voice but nothing prepared me for a very small petite person with a little girl hair-do and exquisite feet.

Dorothy picked me up from L.B.C. Studios and I invited her to lunch. We played the album and she cried all the way through my recording of 'I'll See You Again' because it reminded her of Roger. She insisted, although I tried to refuse, to go to her concert. Every year Dorothy takes a theatre to sing to her fans. This year she had taken the Palladium on Guy Fawkes Night, 5 November – the worst night of the year to sell seats in any theatre but the theatre was packed and Dorothy took the roof off. Where that voice came from I can't imagine. During her performance she told the audience that she loved my album of love songs and asked them all to sing 'If You Were the Only Girl in the World' to me as I sat in the Royal Box. She followed it with 'I'll See You Again' with tears in her eyes and then told everyone to buy my album. It was an unbelievable tribute from a professional to an amateur – from one woman to another. Only a Celt could have been so generous in thought, word and deed. On her Christmas card to me she wrote 'No Queen has ever looked as beautiful as you did in the Royal Box. Love Dorothy' – her heart was as big as her voice.

To my knowledge, this was the only Christmas card Dorothy ever sent. I'm sure it was because she thought Dame Barbara could further her career. After that first meeting, Dorothy was often a guest at Barbara Cartland's home for dinner. Marina Monios, a BBC make-up artist and friend of Dorothy's, told me of the time she had accompanied her. Amongst the illustrious guests was Lord Mountbatten. Dorothy, full of her Celtic charm as usual, proceeded to call him 'an old poof'. He didn't seem to take offence though, on the contrary, he roared with laughter.

16

The Final Downfall

Dorothy's life of rubbing shoulders with the rich and famous was about to change. Her predilection for litigation, buying racehorses and promoting her own concerts inevitably led to her downfall. She owed hundreds of thousands of pounds and in March 1987 she was made bankrupt and evicted from her beautiful home at Bray. Dorothy hated paying bills, even when she *had* money. When the overdue bill for the rates arrived, she had headed notepaper printed with the headline 'Shit' emblazoned across it. She wrapped the money in the paper and tied it to the door knocker for them to collect. Emily remembers the humiliation of crawling about the kitchen on all fours after being ordered to hit the deck when Dorothy spotted the electricity man. He was coming to read the meter because it hadn't been registering any units. Dorothy didn't have any ready money to pay the bill so Des had used a screwdriver with a duster around the blade, so as not to make marks, in order to bypass the system – she was lucky she was never found out.

Dorothy was soon back in court, this time having received an order against her for £7,000 in unpaid taxes. She went berserk; shouting at the judge that she had assets of over a million but the Inland Revenue had refused to accept her cheque. 'My house in Bray is worth five hundred thousand,' she yelled. 'My cottage in Ascot is worth forty thousand, I have three hundred thousand pounds worth of furniture and antiques, forty thousand in jewels and furs and a hundred and ten thousand in gilts.' But Dorothy's protestations were ignored and she was forbidden to issue any more cheques, her assets were frozen and the official receiver was ordered to handle her estate. In 1982 Dorothy received a letter from Stoy Hayward, the London accountants, who were acting for the official receiver in overseeing the administration of her bankruptcy. It informed her that a final general meeting of her creditors was to be held on 27 March. She immediately issued a writ against Stoy Hayward and Hocking. In usual Dorothy style, the writ was a rambling rant, accusing them of things that occurred before their trusteeship began. She even said that they were liable for her bankruptcy, which was ludicrous, as the court had appointed them. The writ was dismissed and costs were awarded against Dorothy; yet one more nail in her litigious coffin.

On 1 April 1982, Dorothy, dressed in a black split skirt and black leather boots, was at a press conference for her forthcoming concert at the newly opened Barbican Centre in London. She told the reporters that she was quitting Britain to live and work in America:

> I've been forced out of this country by nepotism in the theatre and television and the hounding of the press. I don't want anyone to think that I have been beaten so I am going out with a bang. I will star in one last London concert, when I open the new 2,000-seat Barbican Concert Hall on April the 13th.
>
> Straight after the show I plan to fly to Los Angeles where I have been promised financial backing for my stage musical 'Old Rowley' based on the life of Charles the Second.

This was the first concert Dot had done in London for three years; the previous one had to be cancelled because the Inland Revenue had frozen her assets. When pressed by the reporters on how she was going to fund the concert, in view of her forthcoming bankruptcy, she exploded:

I'm being paid a great deal of money for this and l will be putting most of the money back into my show. I have booked a 66-piece orchestra and will be buying two beautiful new gowns. It will cost a fortune but what the hell; I want to make sure that the fans who love me get value for money.

When the fans found out about Dorothy's intended farewell concert, the box office was inundated with calls and the show was a great success. Needless to say Dorothy didn't leave the country and her bankruptcy case rumbled on for years. The final general meeting of her creditors was held on 27 March 1988. They included Barbara Mandell, an agent Dorothy owed money to for the backing singer's she'd booked for the Palladium show. This started the ball rolling. Dorothy was refusing to pay her, insisting that the singers had been booked as a self-contained act and not as musicians. The paltry sum she owed Barbara was the least of her worries, she also owed British Gas, Green Piggott, Scott Worall & Co., J.M. Orchestra Management, Allied Irish Bank, Inland Revenue – the list was endless. Suffice it to say she owed in excess of £300,000. The bailiffs took everything, right down to bottles of wine and champagne that Danny La Rue had presented to her at her London Palladium concert. She was heartbroken. Dorothy still insisted she had the money to pay. Her gilts, pensions and her house and cottage in Windsor, the sale of which would more than cover her debts, and still leave enough for her to live comfortably. But the misguided and, should I say, bloody-mindedness not to pay Barbara Mandell led ultimately to her being evicted from her Thames-side mansion. Dorothy described the scene of her traumatic departure to me in graphic detail:

I'll never forget that day, it was bitterly cold but beautiful; the snowdrops were peeping through a dusting of frost which covered my lawn that swept down to the banks of the river. I'd been tipped off that the bailiffs were coming so I was in my bedroom trying to stuff as many clothes and jewellery as I could into a suitcase before they arrived. I managed to hurl them out of the window just before they turned up. They were like the bloody Gestapo marching across the lawn with their heavy boots; they didn't give a fuck about crushing my fragile flowers, the heartless bastards. The one carrying a battering ram proceeded to break the door down. When I heard it give way I heaved the last cases out of the window. The bailiffs, followed by six policemen, spilled into the hall and swarmed up the stairs. One of them burst into my bedroom and handed me a writ. I flung it back in his face and told him to get out of my house – didn't he have anything better to do than throw people into the street for a living – the prick! Then the cops grabbed me and I was frogmarched down the stairs, kicking and screaming like a common criminal. They half dragged half carried me into the street. I stumbled and fell, scagging my knees on the gravel path. My tights were torn, my knees were bleeding and they just left me there, squatting on all fours, watching the sadistic bastards padlocking the door and securing the windows of my lovely house. I had to book into the Riviera Hotel at Maidenhead.

This was Dorothy's romantic version of what happened that day but in fact Des and Peter, accompanied by Douggie Darnell, helped Dorothy to clear the house before the bailiffs turned up. Douggie took the stage clothes for safe keeping. Dorothy had already purloined the jewellery and her mink coats and given them to Peter to look after.

The requisition of the house more than covered any debts that she had and she was allowed to keep her furniture. The bailiffs said they would send it to any address for free, but Dorothy, for some delusional reason, refused to believe that she wouldn't get her house back, furniture and all. Some of the furniture could have gone to Christies; they wanted fourteen items including a refectory table and the French wardrobe, which was the twin to the one owned by Princess Grace of Monaco. The sale would have given Dorothy much-needed funds but she ignored the offer and the furniture was sent to the Reading Business Centre for storage.

A family trip to Tenby, South Wales. Top right is Rene, Dorothy's sister, with her husband George. Dorothy aged 15, is sat in front, hand on head; directly in front of her is her brother Fred and in front of him is Archie, Dorothy's father. (Emily Squires Private Collection)

Dorothy on stage with her mentor and first love, Billy Reid, the band leader and composer. (Emily Squires Private Collection)

Dorothy returning from New York on the *Queen Mary*. Sat opposite, eating, is her brother Fred who's sat next to Billy Reid. (Emily Squires Private Collection)

Publicity shot *c.* 1948. (Emily Squires Private Collection)

Dorothy dancing with her brother Fred before his sad demise aged 37. (Emily Squires Private Collection)

Dorothy in her dressing room preparing to go on stage with, from left to right: Joyce Golding, her sister-in-law, and centre, Rex Jameson aka Mrs Shufflewick. (Emily Squires Private Collection)

A musical soirée at St Mary's Mount. Dorothy sings accompanying herself on the ukulele, Tony Osborn, her musical arranger, is at the piano and Roger is joining in on guitar. (George Douglas [deceased])

Dorothy and Roger relaxing in her bar at St Mary's Mount. (Alamy stock photo)

Emily with her mother and
Auntie Dorothy on the beach
at Brighton. (Emily Squires
Private Collection)

Dorothy and Roger arriving
home from New York with
a present for Emily. She kept
it for years until its head fell
off. (Emily Squires Private
Collection)

SUNDAY
DECEMBER 6th
One Performance only
at 7.30

LONDON
PALLADIUM
ARGYLL ST. W.1.

—— IN CONCERT ——

DOROTHY SQUIRES

Recording a Live L.P. from
the Stage of the London Palladium
with

THE JOHNNY HOWARD BAND

SIMON OATES ✱ **STAN STENNETT**
STAR OF DOOMWATCH   WALES' ZANY COMEDIAN

JOHNNY GRAY ✱ **JOHNNY TUDOR**
The World's Greatest Saxophonist   Winner of the Knokke Song Festival

Recording under the Direction of NICKY WELSH

PRICES OF ADMISSION
Stalls 20/- 30/- 40/-   Royal Circle 20/- 30/- 40/-
Upper Circle 10/6 15/-   Boxes 60/- 120/- 160/-

Dorothy and Roger returning home after
another trip to the USA. (Emily Squires
Private Collection)

The playbill of Dorothy's comeback
concert at the world famous London
Palladium. (Emily Squires Private
Collection)

Dorothy in a jubilant mood in her dressing room after her successful comeback concert at the London Palladium. (Emily Squires Private Collection)

Dorothy planting a smacker on Norman Newell, her recording manager, at a fundraising event at the Grosvenor Hotel in London. (Emily Squires Private Collection)

Dorothy in New York before her concert at the Carnegie Hall on 22 October 1972. (Emily Squires Private Collection)

Dorothy on tour, pictured with Johnny Tudor at the Capitol Theatre Cardiff in 1971. (The *South Wales Echo*)

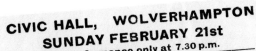

CIVIC HALL, WOLVERHAMPTON
SUNDAY FEBRUARY 21st
One performance only at 7.30 p.m.

LONDON'S LATEST SMASH HIT PALLADIUM SHOW

DOROTHY SQUIRES

with KENNY BROWN (pianist)

Featuring the
TONY EVANS ORCHESTRA

under the direction of NICKY WELSH, musical director
to Dorothy Squires and producer of
"MY WAY" and all her other hits.

Also featuring

The Sensational Sound of

Tommy GODFREY
"Arnold" Star of Popular
Yorkshire T. V. Series "On the House"

Johnny GRAY
The World's Greatest
Saxophonist

JOHNNY TUDOR

Winner 1970 Knokke and Gibraltar
Song Festivals

Prices of Admission £1.50 (£1-10-0) £1.05 (£1-1-0) 53p. (10/6)

To:- Wolverhampton Civic Hall

Please send me............tickets value............Cheque / P.O.

for............enclosed

Name............

Address............

Printed by Hourdsprint Stafford

The playbill for one of the tour dates. (Emily Squires Private Collection)

Dorothy at home in Bexley answering her fan mail. (Emily Squires Private Collection)

Dorothy working out her routine for a forthcoming concert. (Emily Squires Private Collection)

Dorothy writing her lighting plot for her second Palladium concert. (Emily Squires Private Collection)

St Mary's Mount, Bexley.
Dorothy's beautiful
home, which tragically
burnt to the ground.
(Emily Squires Private
Collection)

Dorothy at home in
happier days at Bexley.
(Emily Squires Private
Collection)

Dorothy in cabaret with Kenny Brown at the piano. (Emily Squires Private Collection)

Letter sent to Emily, pleading for her to come home after one of their many bust ups. (Emily Squires Private Collection)

From left to right: Emily Squires, Dorothy and her secretary Hilda Brown on their way to one of her many court cases. (Emily Squires Private Collection)

Emily, Dennis Lotus and Dorothy on their way to court to fight an action against Weston Taylor of the *Sunday Express* for an article they printed entitled 'When Love Turned Sour'. (Emily Squires Private Collection)

Dorothy escaping a flood as Peter Bennett, Hilda Brown, Betty Newman and Des Brown look on. (Emily Squires Private Collection)

Dorothy's Thames-side home at Bray – purported to have been built for Lilly Langtree by her lover King Edward VII. (Emily Squires Private Collection)

Dorothy speaking Welsh to her beloved racehorses: Norwegian Flag, Esban and Walberswick, as her dog Esban II looks on. (Emily Squires Private Collection)

Dorothy with Norwegian Flag before he was tragically brought down in a race and had to be put down. (Emily Squires Private Collection)

17

Homeless

Now, homeless for the first time in her life, she called all her old friends for help. She rang Ben, her builder friend from Bexley. He said she could stay with him but didn't know what his wife Robina would think about it – Dorothy was asked to leave after only two weeks. The term 'fair-weather friends' couldn't have been more apt; where were the sycophantic hangers on now, who were there for the good times? Hilda, who'd been her closest confidant and secretary for years, refused to put her up, saying she had no room; Betty, her old school friend, whom she'd brought to London and given a home in St Mary's Mount, refused to open the door. Dorothy had to suffer the indignity of having to communicate with her through the letter box.

Even her own sister, Rene, turned her away. She didn't have the guts to tell her herself so she sent George, her husband, who kept her on the doorstep insisting they had no room. Dorothy knew this to be a barefaced lie. Eventually she found refuge in a room above an antique shop that had no toilet or running water. She dossed there until she moved into the Riviera

Hotel in Maidenhead, where she stayed for about six months. The ever loyal, Peter, on returning from a holiday in Tunisia, went to the hotel and asked to see her. He was immediately summoned to the manager's office. Trouble was afoot. He was told in no uncertain manner that they wanted Dorothy out. 'But she's got nowhere to go,' he pleaded. 'I want her out,' the manager continued, 'she's become very demanding and abusive and I have to think of the other guests.'

At her wits' end, Dorothy decided to make an appointment to see the Housing Officer at Windsor in the hope he could provide her with accommodation. She succeeded in getting an interview with the housing officer and so Peter, one of her few remaining loyal friends, accompanied her to the meeting. Peter recalls:

Dorothy got herself all dressed up to the nines for the interview, she looked lovely. I drove her to Windsor. We arrived a bit early for the meeting so I suggested we go across the road to the Castle Hotel. Des and I would often go there for morning coffee with our friend Arnie, you know? Anyway, while we waited for our coffee some Christmas carols came over the P.A. system, it was almost Christmas you see. Well, if it did, Dorothy broke down sobbing; she was breaking her heart … It broke my heart to see what she had come to. 'Why have they done this to me, Peter,' she said. 'They've taken everything; my house in Bray, my cottage in Windsor, my gilts, my horses, my furniture, everything.' Don't upset yourself Dot I said, it'll be ok; I'm sure the council will give you somewhere to live. But I couldn't have been more wrong. The housing officer said he was sorry for her predicament but all he could offer her was a refuge, sharing with abandoned and battered wives with their babies. Come on Dot I said let's go, this is not for you and I drove her back to the Riviera Hotel.

She knew she couldn't pay her bill so she decided to do a runner. Peter offered to pay but she refused. She ordered him to take the car to the back of the hotel and wait. Peter was soon faced with the incongruous scenario of a former superstar, dressed in a full-length mink coat clambering down the fire escape like a thief in the night.

I can only imagine what Dorothy must have been going through, this icon, who'd been admired by her peers, loved by her fans and rubbed shoulders with royalty. Where were they now; where were the freeloaders she'd been so generous to and where was the family that she'd subsidised all through the good times? Homeless once again, she decided to break back into her house. She called her friend Mike Terry, and with his help and a man called David, they proceeded to break in. It wasn't going to be easy, all the locks had been changed but Dorothy knew of a window that she could get through. So, with the help of the boys she clambered through a small window at the back of the house, no small feat for a 70-plus woman. She was horrified at what confronted her. Her once beautiful home was a shambles, there was rubbish everywhere, the toilets had been used and not flushed; it was as if squatters had been using it. Even though the gas and electricity had been cut off, Dorothy and Mike barricaded themselves in and prepared for siege. Dorothy spent what was to be the loneliest Christmas of her life with only candles for light and warmth.

She was in dire straits when she received a lifeline; a letter that contained a cheque for £11,275.86 and an apology for the delay caused by problems with arranging the transfer of funds. The letter had been forwarded from the Riviera Hotel. It was from Harbottle and Lewis, a London-based law firm that specialised in media who were acting for Roger. Dorothy's mind was obviously starting to go by this time as her ramblings in her letter of reply highlight. Nevertheless, they throw up some intriguing scenarios; was this part of her divorce settlement or was Roger still supporting his ex-wife? I'll let *you* decide. The following is part of the letter that Dorothy wrote to his lawyer:

North Wing
Fishery Road
Bray Berks
24-2-1988

Your Ref: 2/DSK
Harbottle &Lewis
34 South Melton Street
London W1P 2BP

Dear Sir,

I went to see Dennis Sellinger as I know he was Roger's agent and, Dennis was a friend of many years standing, notwithstanding the fact that I did not want Roger saddled with your fees, moreover you are aware of the job that was done on Roger R.E. the book that Roy Mosley fronted in 1985, you surely recall me telephoning you and even read you parts of the book; that book was written to finish Roger. I warned you on no account should that book be read by Roger's parents, especially his mother.

Despite the fact that you write in your letter on the 15 February 1988, that 'no acknowledgement or receipt is required' really Mr Stutter, what kind of person would I be not to acknowledge and thank Roger for the sum of £11, 27586. You wrote that Roger apologises for the delay in forwarding the remittance, which apparently was caused by difficulties in making arrangements over the transfer of funds. I would expect the balance of the £25, 000 that I so desperately begged for many weeks ago, and not to encumber the transfer problem I am prepared to accept the balance in Dollars, thus avoiding whatever charges are incurred by the conversion charges from dollars to pounds, and would you please inform me of the sum incurred re the conversion charges, as referred to in your 3rd para of your letter of the 15th inst.

I moved out of the Thames Riviera on the 9 February and returned to my home North Wing. I had of course written to the high court informing them of my intentions and requested police protection. The management of that super hotel, Thames Riviera sent on the parcel of mail, as I said I would be around to collect my mail but I have been so very very busy. I did not receive the mail from the Thames Riviera until yesterday, the 23rd and your letter and cheques were among the many letters, and all good news, legally I mean.

Mr Stutter, do you recall me calling you on the 9 December 1987? I was telephoning from the Royal Courts of Justice. I was due before the Honourable Justice Owen, as he asked me to make an affidavit, I heartily agreed so I sat up until 430 a.m. to write my affidavit in long hand, swore it in the following morning, and all ready for the Justice Owen. I telephoned you requesting the bank in Jersey where Roger had made a deposit re the divorce settlement of £50,000.

As you are aware that a Mr Raymond Hocking, in the role of Ultra Varies Trustee was up to his eyes in the conspiracy quagmire, according to his affidavit that he swore on the 26 May 1987, for an order so that I hand over the keys of my home within 28 days of the order of the 15 September 1987. Suffice it to say the affidavit will hang him and a great many more. I telephoned you from the Royal Courts of Justice, as Mr Raymond Hocking had sworn in his affidavit that I had a bank account in Jersey. I needed the name of the only bank account that I was aware of was the bank that Roger had deposited the agreed sum of £50,000.

After many years of subterfuge, the workings of you and your contemporaries, Darlington and Nice must be dealt with.

I want the name of that bank in Jersey and I want some answers as to why Roger paid me in instalments, and even swore an affidavit, that either you or your contemporaries drew up and swear an affidavit of means, a matter of five weeks after he was married. I want the reasons as to why, after many letters to my solicitor, I received a cheque for £18,000 from Roger.

Some 18 months later, after many letters and phone calls from me, I received £25,000. Mr Stutter, I want the name of that bank as I want my accountant to investigate to investigate the situation. When reading Roger's affidavit of means, wherein he swore that he could not get a divorce except on prohibitive terms that was the worst part. I now realise that Roger was guided very carefully, which I'm sure at the time, he welcomed, as Roger has never been generous to say the least. My fault, I never asked for money off him.

There are another four pages of this rant, which I won't subject you to but reading between the lines as one has to with Dorothy, the upshot of this letter is she was accusing people of conspiracy, denying that she was ever made bankrupt, denying that she had a bank account in Jersey, asking for answers as to why Roger paid her divorce settlement in instalments and insinuating that in his affidavit Roger was pleading poverty; ironic when you think his settlement with Luisa was £10 million.

Even Dorothy's tenacity, however misguided, had to yield to the forces of bureaucracy in the end and she was evicted once more from her home in Bray.

Now, homeless for the second time, she was given refuge in Port Talbot by Des and Peter with whom she stayed for two and a half years. For a while she seemed settled and even thought about working again. Des, thinking he was helping, suggested that he could act as her agent and book her to do a concert at the Grand Theatre in Swansea. Dorothy agreed and the wheels were put in motion. As the time drew nearer no one could find her. Des, now her interim manager, was inundated with over 200 phone calls.

An irate Sean Kier, the manager of the theatre, phoned Des and told him that unless he received confirmation and the contract he sent Dorothy six weeks previously, he would have to cancel the sell-out concert. The long-suffering Des hadn't heard from Dot in weeks and had no idea where she was. He informed Mr Kier that as far as he was concerned he was no longer acting as her manager. Dorothy eventually returned but the situation couldn't last. Dorothy wasn't the easiest of people to live with at the best of times and Des, however good a friend, couldn't take it anymore. Des was in failing health so Peter, the younger of the two, offered to look after her. He decided to rent a house in Swansea. It was a lovely house with a swimming pool; this was more Dorothy's style. So Peter, Dorothy and Peter's Labrador Benson moved in.

Dorothy seemed settled for a while but true to form it didn't last. She became more obsessive and paranoid. When she heard that a prisoner had escaped from Swansea jail, she was convinced he was out to get her and began sticking newspaper and record covers over all the windows. Peter, for all his good intentions, soon found out that he'd bitten off more than he could chew. The last straw came when Benson, his Labrador, was taken ill. Peter didn't know what was wrong with him; he was staggering about as if he was drunk. It transpired that he'd eaten half of Dorothy's cache of Purple Hearts and was as high as a kite. This caused a bit of a rift between Dot and Peter and not long after, she decided to leave.

Once again she contacted the Windsor and Maidenhead Council, in the hope that they would relent and provide her with a council flat. She sent them this heartfelt, if somewhat confused, letter. There is some logic to it, as she tried to make a case for herself but you will see by its contents that her mind was wandering. Goodness knows what some unsuspecting clerk in the council office made of this epistle:

REF: Dorothy Squires Homeless
37 Sitwell Way
Port Talbot
West Glamorgan
South Wales 15/12/1990

Executive Chief Clerk
Town Hall
Royal Windsor and Maidenhead Council
31 St Ives Road
Maidenhead, Berks

Dear Sir/Madam

I have been homeless since I was evicted at 9.45 a.m.
on 1 December 1987 from my home in North Wing Fisheries
Road Bray Berks. At the time of my eviction the
bailiff, Mr Brian Ripley of Slough County Court, the
representative of Raymond Hocking of Messrs Stoy
Hayward, advised me to seek Council accommodation. Since
my eviction I have moved five times and the situation
is such that I am compelled to move yet again; I would
appreciate a three-bedroom apartment, having lived in
Bray from October 1974 to 1 December 1987, thus being a
ratepayer for thirteen years and one month, would make
me eligible for accommodation off the council.

I understand that all my chattels, personal
belongings, my expensive and expansive wardrobe, my
beautiful antique furniture etc. are stored somewhere
in Reading, Berks. I of course realise that my antique
furniture would be too large to fit into a council
apartment but the tools of my trade, my piano and my
recording equipment, would fit into a council apartment.
In any event I understand my furniture has been sold,

according to Messrs Booth and Blackwell, solicitors for
Raymond Hocking, who was appointed judicial trustee
on 29 October 1986 by the Slough County Court by a
Mr G. Hawks, an authorised officer of the department of
Trade and Industry who arranged the sale of my home.
Be that as it may, I will make do with rugs on the
floor, a bed, a few chairs, and a kitchen. But I do need
the tools of my trade around me so that I can sing and
perform, do the things I was born to do.

I enclose a copy of the *Stage and Television Weekly*,
Friday 22 February, containing the heraldry of my
concert at the 2400-seater Dome theatre in Brighton.
I also enclose a copy of the *Sunday Telegraph* 18 March.
My concert was on the 17 March. Normally the prices of
the tickets are five or six pounds but as you will note
the prices of the tickets for my concert were £15, £16,
and £9.50 and it was a sell out, as stated in the *Sunday
Telegraph*. It also stated in the stated article, my
devoted fans paid £1,000 for an advert on the back page
of the *Stage* and I wasn't even aware of what they had
planned. The photograph of me in a rowing boat was just
after I moved into my house, North Wing, Fisheries Road,
Bray, and the gown that I'm wearing in the photo with
Danny La Rue is a gown of Mr La Rue; a copy of one of
mine, he wore when he impersonated me.

The article in the *Sunday Telegraph* of course somewhat
oblique but at least they had to report it was a sell
out and I may add many many many were turned away, but
the article by Megan Tresidder is biased, and quite
quite untrue, but one doesn't quibble at these issues
one grins and bears them. There is one issue I take
umbrage with and I quote: 'And the moment she walked

out of court having won £30,000 from the *News of the World* only to be confronted by her creditors.' Megan Tresiddder is right about winning £30,000 damages from the *News of the World* but Megan omitted to add there was ten and a half years cost awarded to me re the *News of the World* Trial was on the 15 to 26 June 1981, and Rupert Murdoch has not paid the £30,000 damages nor have I ever received the ten and a half years costs ordered by the court.

On 26 June 1981, and Megan Tresiddder was also wrong when she wrote 'only to be confronted by her creditors,' I had no creditors. Moreover, Megan Tresidder writes at penultimate paragraph of fourth column under purported quotes from Mr Lloyd: 'The Welsh Dragon is breathing fire again' (but dear Megan must have a cruel sense of innuendo to say) 'As the fans boarded the coaches to take them to Brighton, towards songs like 'I Know a Millionaire' and 'The Man That Got Away' – I don't even know the song, 'I Know a Millionaire' – I do know 'The Man That Got Away' but it was not sung by me on the 17 March 1990; Roger Moore is a millionare and the man that got away, but I seem to be the only one that's divorced her husband, but the press will never let it die, for me at least.'

But to combat this Megan Tresiddder, I enclose the front page of the *Brighton Evening Argus*. I had been searching for Johnny Gray, one of the greatest exponents of the saxophone in the world, and a great artiste. I heard about this article, I telephoned the Brighton Argus For Mr Gray's telephone number, on 17 March 1990 1 arranged that Johnny Gray do his own spot, he blew out 'Stardust' aid paralysed the audience, he was terrific,

he also was on stage in my two hour act end blew that
SAX and boy what a differnece he made, The orchestra
was first class anyway a great great sound in today's
Synthesizer age.

That concert on 17 March 1990 earned several hundred
pounds re, the tax on the tickets, several hundreds
in VAT for the Treasury, at least a hundred people
were employed, composing of theatre staff, and more
important than this there were twenty musicians and two
acts working that night, and this was my first concert
for six years, when I opened the Giant Barbican Theatre
on 12 April 1982 I mounted a 62-piece orchestra and
eight male singers, the theatre of 2,400 was packed, I
paid the VAT that date on nine hundred pounds, Musical
Director and my own accompanist 72 musicians were
employed, and that being the reason I want the council
to furnish me with apartment.

I want to present my concerts as I have always done,
mount orchestras, give acts work, make many people
happy, earn money for the VAT end Tax, make the treasury
more money but I cannot unless I get Into a home. I
can practice, write songs, motivate and arrange the
musical scores. I spent five weeks rehearsing by playing
recordings of the songs I was to sing on the 17 March
1990, I had to travel by train to Paddington carting
cases of music, having many hours sorting out my
music library.

The preparation of the concert of the 17 March 1990,
was a tremendous task, that being the reason I went
to live in Maidenhead so that my pianist and musical
director can come to a place that I can call my own.
In retrospect my Stage gowns are stored in London -

I want my gowns to be where I am living. There are 31
gowns in all, each costing in excess of £2,000, so I
would appreciate suitable accommodation as soon as
possible please. I have always been known as one of
the best-dressed stars and all my clothes are rotting
in some store. I have handbags and dozens of shoes
matching, suits and dresses. All I have now are a few
things I was allowed to take out of my home and, as God
is my judge, one of my suitcases was taken when I went
to telephone for a taxi. I had to rely on Oxfam but at
least it did some good buying from Oxfam. I have always
had a talent for designing and making dresses, suits
etc. So, with needle and thread, I turned the Oxfam
leftovers into Cinderella's Honeymoon gear. Suffice it
to say, I often wonder if this 'er United Kingdom is a
democracy.

Yours faithfully,
Dorothy Squires

She didn't succeed in her quest to get a council flat and this once feisty, proud
woman was reduced to living on the charity of others. At her wits end, she
turned to the only man she had really ever loved for support, in the vain hope
that he would help her dire situation. She sent a letter to Roger but alas her
plea fell on deaf ears and who could blame him; Dorothy was well in his past,
after all, he'd had another wife and three children since then.

You might be forgiven for thinking that she brought all this misfortune on
herself, but you would be wrong; no one knew it at the time but Dorothy
was ill. Not with the cancer that was to bring down the final curtain on this
remarkable woman's life but a mental illness, which had been compounded
by her habit of perpetually popping Purple Hearts. Emily Squires and I are

convinced that she was suffering from bipolar, all her life. She had all the symptoms; when she was high she would become very extravagant, buying racehorses, funding record sessions, promoting her own concerts etc. But when she was down she wouldn't leave the house, staying in bed all day and slopping about in her dressing gown.

This behaviour would try the patience of even the most loyal of friends and Peter, one of the devoted, was on the verge of a nervous breakdown. But fate took a hand; Doris Joyce, the wife of the owner of a nightclub called the Ace of Clubs in Leeds, came to her rescue, offering Dorothy the use of a cottage she owned. So, Dorothy moved up north and I, along with Emily, lost contact with her for almost eight years. Many people have criticised Emily for not doing more, which is an unfair evaluation. Dorothy wouldn't give anyone her telephone number but from time to time she would call Emily. She wouldn't tell her where she was living. However, Emily did eventually find her address and sent her this letter:

Hove, Sussex
21.9.95

Dear Auntie Dorothy,
It was good to hear from you the other night. I enclose the book about Roger. Mum says there is no need to return it so you can read it at your leisure. Take care of yourself and don't forget to send me your telephone number so I can phone you.
I love you, look after yourself, Emily Jane xxxxx

During her stay in Leeds, she was reunited with her friend Mike Terry who lived nearby in Kettlethorp. She seemed to rely quite heavily upon him, even giving him power of attorney for all her banking needs. Mike was obsessed with Dorothy. Knowing Dot as I did, I could see how one could become obsessed with her; she was a very charismatic character but Mike booking a number of theatres, one being Her Majesty's' Theatre in London, to do a tribute show was a step too far. When Dorothy found out, she was furious. She told me that Mike was doing all her songs and using all her arrangements. 'He's a pianist and a bloody good one,' she said, 'but he's not a bloody singer; he'll bring my name into disrepute.' She wasn't wrong either; the show was a disaster. Patrick Newley described the event in the *Newley of the Stage* newspaper:

A CONTROVERSIAL tribute show to legendary Welsh singer Dorothy Squires returns to Wales this week. Entertainer Mike Terry will be impersonating the star at the Grand Pavilion in Porthcawl. But when he staged his show in London's West End two years ago it proved to be a flop. Critics branded the performance as 'grotesque' and claimed about 20 people left Her Majesty's Theatre while Terry was on stage. 'Mr Terry neither looks nor sounds even remotely like Miss Squires,' said theatre critic Patrick Newley at the time. 'The only word that comes to mind to describe his performance is grotesque. Judging by the number of people who walked out while he was on stage, it appeared that Dorothy's fans were not exactly impressed.'

After this disaster Mike even contemplated repeating this undignified performance at the London Palladium. I think he thought he *was* Dorothy, dressed in plumes of purple ostrich feathers, and singing her songs, but there was only one Dot. Dorothy was running out of money again; she hadn't applied for a state pension, either because she was too proud or perhaps it was because she had always knocked ten years off her age. She'd even tippexed her age out of her passport and now didn't want to own up. Either way she was in need of funds to pay her council tax so, at the age of 75, she decided to come out of retirement for one last time. Dorothy's final concert was at the Brighton Dome in March 1990. She made her final appearance in front of a house full of her devoted fans. It was an ignominious performance; Dorothy was very nervous. It had been a while since she'd performed and some of the lyrics she'd sung a thousand times now eluded her. She was a shadow of the performer she had once been. Emily was in the audience that night. She told me that it was one of the most harrowing experiences of her life. She was chewing her raincoat, metaphorically speaking, hoping that Dot could reach the notes that once thrilled her audiences.

If nothing else, Dot was a pro. She battled on and when she sailed into the medley of her hits, she had the audience in the palm of her hand. The fans rose as they once did and gave her a standing ovation. Tony Ortzen, a critic from the *The Stage* newspaper, wrote:

THE STAGE AND TELEVISION TODAY March 29 1990

RARELY can the Dome have seen a night like it for this was vintage Squires, the put-to-one-side Bollinger for a special occasion. Wearing a £2,000 burned orange-coloured chiffon and ostrich feather evening gown, Squires, the Grande Dame of the dramatic, swept on to the stage – and received a spontaneous and rapturous standing ovation … without singing a single word. Squires does not just show a little of her soul, unselfconsciously, she strips it positively naked to sing of past amours, of life's tragedies, triumphs and turmoil. But the sheer joy of it is that she'll also send herself up too, and is the first to do so if she misses a line or two.

The atmosphere was almost like that of a Revivalist meeting, with Squires the golden haired goddess the faithful went to worship. Some travelled many miles to attend, her concerts, sadly, now being relatively few. Indeed, this, a sell out, was her first for six years. In short, it was a gutsy, good natured, exhilarating 100 minutes-plus performance. Garland has long gone, Piaf has passed. But their spirit lives on in Squires, who will belt it out one minute only to dramatically change the temperature – and the tempo – of the evening by switching to a quieter, more intimate and gentle mode.

Pre-concert advertising billed Squires as a 'legend in her lifetime'. For some it would be an overstatement, for others a gross exaggeration, but long may she yet add to that legend. Backed by the Kenny Brown Orchestra, Squires now has her sights set once again on the London Palladium. Once she's there, she'll do it 'My Way'. No, for Squires, it's not just a song, it's her well-deserved anthem.

After thanking the loyal fans she told them that this was her final concert, 'I've only done this in order to pay my Poll Tax,' she said. 'Just think, my husband is probably sipping champagne at home in Switzerland … Oh well!' she sighed. 'That's life I suppose.' Emily went backstage to see Dorothy after the show and was given a very cool reception by Brenda, Dorothy's dresser. Emily hadn't seen Dot in three years, through no fault of her own. Brenda wasn't aware that since Dot had moved to Leeds, she had refused to give anyone her address. Dorothy stayed in Leeds for the next three years, until Doris Joyce finally died and the family wanted to sell the house.

When Dorothy was given notice to quit, John Lloyd, the president of her fan club, contacted Roger asking if he would consider buying the property for her but he declined and Dorothy found herself under threat of eviction once again. The estate manager told her in no mean terms that he'd had instructions from Doris's family to send in the bailiffs and change the locks. Not wanting the humiliation of being evicted for the third time in her life, Dorothy bowed to the inevitable and left of her own accord.

Knowing that she was about to be on the move again, she gave the master tapes of all her recordings to Mike Terry for safe keeping. A bad move as it transpired; Mike misguidedly thought because he had the aforementioned tapes in his possession, he owned the copyright to all her works. Nothing could have been further from the truth and this misunderstanding was to cause considerable consternation after her death. When the news hit the press that Dorothy was homeless again, she received bundles of letters. Some came from nutters, some from genuine fans; she even received this letter from a fan who, though she could little afford it, sent her a £10 note:

Oct 13

33 Whiteleas Way
South Shields
So Tyneside
NE34 8LJ

Dear Miss Squires

I was sorry to hear on Franks broadcast on Sunday how despondent and miserable you feel at the moment. I have always loved to hear you singing. I wish I could help to make you feel better, because there are people who care about you. I myself am a widowed pensioner and you know we get a £10 bonus at Christmas please accept the £10 enclosed I shall get it back at Christmas and I can wait for it. Maybe it will help you with a bill which is pressing. I hope this letter makes you feel better. My favourite song you sing is 'Say It With Flowers'. God bless and help you.

Yours most sincerely
Terese Dutton

From the myriad of letters, Dorothy chose one that came from Esme Coles, offering her the use of a house in Trebanog in the Rhondda Valley. Dorothy told me there was something about the letter that told her it was the right thing to do – it was Wales – she was going home. Esme wrote:

Dear Miss Squires,

I hope you won't think I'm interfering with your privacy but after reading of your circumstances I had to write to you to offer my sincere regrets of your plight.

I have been an ardent admirer of you for many years and have been privileged to have been in your company after your performance at a nightclub in South Wales. I know you won't remember me but I used to have the Hillside Club in Tonyrefail, which I sold a few years ago.

Having a large detached house that is vacant, you would be most welcome to stay there as long as you want to.

I hope that your circumstances change for the better but my offer will always be open to you.

Best regards Esme

18

Back to Wales

After reading the letter from Esme Coles, Dot contacted Mike Terry. He hired a small van, loaded up her belongings and they headed for the Rhondda Valley in South Wales. As the small van wound its way through the slate grey streets of the semi-deserted Welsh valley towns, Dorothy, still in her mink coat and diamante glasses, must have cut an incongruous figure – surrounded by her belongings.

This was a long way from the life she'd been used to; she'd left Wales to get away from all this. Since her eviction in December 1987 from her home in Bray, she had been forced to move fourteen times. The Rhondda Valley was to be her last and it was where she ended her days. Although I'd lost contact with Dorothy after she was evicted from Bray – she'd become a virtual recluse, cut off from most, if not all of her friends and family – it was a fortuitous meeting with John Lloyd that reconnected me with my old friend. Geraint Stanley Jones, the controller of BBC Wales had invited me to Shirley Bassey's Variety Club Tribute at Cardiff City Hall. John Lloyd was there that night. Although he was Dorothy's number one fan he was also a fan of Shirley's, for obvious reasons – they were both Welsh, both divas and John was gay. I asked him if he knew how I could contact Dorothy. Reluctantly he gave me her number in Leeds, the last contact he had for her and he made me promise not to tell her where I'd got it from. She did, however, give it to her first cousin Maggie. She wrote to her on 23 January 1996 and from the tone of the letter it was obvious that Dorothy was feeling nostalgic for the life she had once enjoyed but was now just a distant memory.

My dear Maggie,

It is now 330 a.m. Tuesday. It was great hearing your voice; I had a damn good cry when I hung up. When I recall what they have done to me it is beyond belief. I would appreciate it if you would loan me the photo's you have of my beautiful furniture in my home; North Wing, Fisheries Road, Bray. I will return them to you when I get them copied. My telephone number is ex-directory - so, Maggie don't give it to anybody except Jamie - I spoke to him at length after I called you. Give Jamie my number and my address. If he should call, don't telephone until after 6 p.m. because I won't hear it ring as I'm working upstairs. I will copy this letter for my file, but you can give this letter to Jamie as he has all the dope, or part of what I have been subjected to. I'm writing this on my knee - forgive the scrawl.

God Bless, Maggie. Take care - love and plenty of it. Edna xx

I rang Dorothy the next day but got a very cool reception: 'How did you find me, who told you where I was?' she snapped. 'Never mind all that,' I said, 'I'm ringing to tell you that my father has died.' She went silent for a moment then, with her voice cracking with emotion said, 'My lovely Bert …'

She thanked me for letting her know and told me that she would let me know where she was in due course.

Months went by and I heard nothing. I tried the number in Leeds but it had been discontinued. I tried ringing Emily but she'd changed her number. It was by mere chance that I bumped into Brian Turvey, the producer who'd made the documentary about Dorothy, who told me that Dot was in the BUPA Hospital in Cardiff. This was news to me; Dorothy hadn't been in touch since I'd phoned her. Perhaps she still didn't want people to know where she was but I decided to visit her anyway. I knocked on the door of her private room and went in. She was sat up in bed wearing full make-up, a bed jacket and wearing her ubiquitous diamante encrusted glasses. Suddenly something in the air attacked my nasal passages and I let out a massive sneeze. She squinted over her glasses, fixed me with an icy stare and said, 'Fuck off you'll give me the flu.' 'That's a nice welcome after all these years,' I retorted and we both broke up laughing.

There was so much I wanted to know; where was she living, why she was in hospital, how long had she been back. She told me that she'd been back a couple of months and had been staying with a fan in the Rhondda. She apologised for not getting in touch earlier but she didn't know how long she would be staying. She said she would probably have moved on by now but she was taken ill and rushed in for an operation. It was bladder cancer, but the surgeon had told her that it was 'all in the bucket.' We were talking about old times when the hospital secretary entered the room. She didn't look too happy. She told Dorothy that Roger had only paid for the operation and a limited stay for recuperation, which had expired the week before and there was the matter of a considerable phone bill, which he wasn't liable to pay for. Losing her rag, Dorothy informed the secretary in no mean terms that she wasn't well enough to leave yet and as for the phone bill her husband was a millionaire, so fuck off.

After the woman left, with her tail between her legs, I offered to take Dot back to the Rhondda but she was adamant: 'No,' she said, 'Mike will be taking me back.' She'd put Mike's name down on the pre-admission form as next of kin. She'd also put her date of birth as 1924 when her real date of birth was 1915. She was always knocking years off her age; she'd knocked six years off her marriage certificate, something she regretted now. She'd had hell's own job trying to claim her state pension. I think the reason she didn't want me to take her back to the Rhondda was because she was embarrassed for me to see where she was living and how she had fallen from grace. 'Who is this Esme?' I asked. Dorothy replied:

> She's this fan who offered me her son's house when she heard I was homeless; what she didn't tell me what was that he'd shot his fucking brains out that's why she won't live there; she sleeps in a sleeping bag at the back of her chip shop. If I had known what I know now I wouldn't have come, she won't let anyone near me. I think she only asked me to come here so that she could tell everyone Dorothy Squires was living in her house. I'm like a fucking prisoner; if I ask her to get me any food she leaves it on the doorstep like a dog. I've got nowhere else to go and she knows it. I feel trapped; I don't know if I can face another move, all my stuff is in the house.

But she must have contemplated moving as she wrote in a letter to Dennis Selinger asking for him to forward a letter to Roger: 'I am in a desperate situation as you can see – he is the only one I can turn to – and you are the only one I can rely on.'

I really wanted to find out where she was living so I rang Marina Monios, Dorothy's make-up artist friend. She told me that Dorothy wouldn't give her number to anyone, not even Des and Peter but if I rang Esme she would pass on a message. When Dorothy eventually rang me she sounded very confused, rambling from one subject to another. She was very off-hand and asked me why I wanted to contact her. I told her that I was wondering how she was after her illness. She denied that there was anything wrong with her and started ranting on about Murdoch. She eventually owned up, saying that she was passing blood in her urine. 'But it's only haematuria,' she insisted, 'I've read it in my medical book.' I wasn't convinced so I phoned Doctor Bali, the local GP. She didn't want to tell me anything at first because I wasn't family but when I explained that we were very close friends, she was very sympathetic and told me that unless Dorothy kept her appointments – she'd already cancelled three with the specialist – there was nothing more she could do for her. I decided there was only one thing for it; I had to go to Trebanog.

My heart sank when I pulled onto the pothole-pitted driveway to the side of a chip shop; this was not what Dorothy had been used to at all. A makeshift door made of old tongue-and-groove timber was the only visible entrance. I knocked on the door and was greeted by Esme, a woman of about 60 with blond hair, almost a clone of Dot. The inside of the house did nothing to allay my fears; it was a dog's dinner of a place. The back room of the shop doubled as a living room, bedroom and storeroom. There were boxes of food piled high on the chairs and sideboard, vying incongruously for space with the Capo Di Monte statuettes and family photographs. There was a rumpled sleeping bag on the sofa, where I assume someone slept.

This was not the house that Esme had described in her letter. Esme owned another house in the village, known locally as 'the house of tears', on account of her son who tragically took his own life there. Rumour has it that Esme couldn't face living there after the tragic incident. She offered me tea and told me that having Dorothy wasn't what she'd expected. She'd always loved Dorothy; she loved her records and had seen her many times in concert, but like most fans, she only saw the stage persona. Living with Dorothy had been a very different story; she could be very difficult. Esme told me how to find the house but warned me that Dorothy may not answer the door. At first glance the detached post-war house, standing back off the road, looked rather grand. It was sandwiched between two rows of terraced miner's cottages. A glass loggia ran the whole of the front of house. Spookily, an old red telephone box, similar to the one young Edna May would have changed in, before going on to do her five bob gigs, stood incongruously in the front garden.

As I approached the house, I was aware that all was not what it seemed; there was forlornness about it. There were cracks in the pathway and most of the windows were covered up with old newspapers. I knocked on the door.

A voice from within yelled 'Go away I'm busy.' 'Come on Dot,' I pleaded, 'it's me, Johnny, open the door.' She opened the door a crack, then, seeing that it really was me, reluctantly let me in. I wasn't prepared for the sad sight that greeted me. Dorothy was dressed in an old brown threadbare towelling dressing gown and her feet were clad in torn cotton socks and shabby slippers. I glanced back at the phone box in the garden and thought how different her life had become since she changed in an identical phone box back in Llanelli. I asked why she was living like this. She said she had no choice; she had nowhere else to go. 'Of course you've got a choice,' I said. 'You've only to do a couple of concerts and you would have enough money to rent somewhere decent. The fans would turn out for you I know they would.' She looked at me, tears welled up in her eyes and then she said something I never thought I would hear her say, 'I can't sing anymore, John.'

It filled me with sadness as I compared the broken woman before me with the international star she once was. I gazed around the dreary curtain-less room; it was a shambles. There was an old Dansette gramophone on the floor, a pile of Dorothy Squire's albums stood next to it and old concert posters, scrapbooks and framed signed photos of Dorothy in concert were strewn about haphazardly.

I followed her as she shuffled towards the kitchen. An old Rank Xerox photocopier stood incongruously next to the sink and the kitchen table was piled high with old tabloids and legal documents. 'Make me a hot cup of tea will you, John?' she said. Then, ignoring me, she grabbed a handful of newspapers and started to copy them as if her life depended on it. Every one of the papers had something about her on it. It was as if she was trying to chronicle her life before it was too late. Amongst the papers was an article that Dorothy had written in her halcyon days. I was intrigued to know why she had kept it all these years. Was it to remind her of the good times or was it nostalgia for a simpler life back in the little Welsh village where she was born? I'll let you be the judge:

MY HOME I WORKED FOR
By Dorothy Squires

I was born in a caravan in Bridge-shop field, Pontyberem, a little mining village in South Wales. My parents were fairground people, which is actually another tentacle of show business. For no reason that I can fathom, and much to my sadness, they decided to give up this glorious show life to live in a house. At the time I was much too young to differ but in my own mind I was convinced that I had been born into a great and exciting life, which I intended to pursue and hopefully be successful.

From a telephone booth where I used to change my evening gown years ago to my home in St Mary's Mount, where I live today, was a tough climb with rough roads all the way. That's why I feel there's no business like show business. Admittedly I can only live in my home about sixteen weeks of the year owing to my having to tour the provincial theatres, but when I grab the last train out of Glasgow, Newcastle or Liverpool on a Saturday night, I lie in my sleeper with a sense of satisfaction thinking of my early days spent in a caravan in Wales and knowing that I'm going to my home; the home I worked for; the home I used to dream about as a child. I compare the cramped quarters that were with the freedom I have now, just walking through my orchard and garden of three acres or changing into my swimming costume and bathing in my pool. This was my ambition, which I worked so hard to achieve. My success in show business is linked with numerous people; people who have helped me to achieve these ambitions. There are far too many to mention – but if you are one of them, regardless of whatever little you did, I want to thank you from the bottom of my heart because without you I would probably still be living in that little valley town.

Yours sincerely Dorothy Squires

When I asked her why she was copying all this stuff she said she was suing the paracetamol company because she'd become addicted to painkillers and she needed to copy the information for the trial. It seemed that Dorothy was still obsessed with litigation. Then, brandishing a copy of the *Daily Express*, she screamed, 'I had nothing to do with this.' The *Express* had somehow found out about Dorothy's plight and ran an article in the 'Hickey Column' about Dorothy's illness and Roger paying the bill. She was hysterical. 'What will Roger think,' she wailed. Then, grabbing the phone she frantically dialled Dennis Selinger, Roger's agent at ICM. She was crying and almost incoherent as she pleaded with him not to believe the article; it had nothing to do with her, she cried, and what would Roger think. In truth I don't think she gave a damn what Roger thought; she was more worried that he wouldn't pay the extra bill she'd run up at BUPA.

Swansea – Cosmetic Surgery Ward

A few weeks later Dorothy rang me; she was hysterical. She needed to go to Swansea for an operation to have a mole removed from her face and Esme was refusing to take her. 'I can't let Roger see me like this,' she said. It was amazing, she was more worried about her appearance and the unlikely chance that she would ever see Roger again, than the cancer she was suffering. I arrived in Trebanog with my mother to find Dot experiencing a full-on nosebleed. She was a pitiful sight. A swab from a previous operation had been left up her nose for years and had come away during the bleed. The two-piece suit she was wearing, which looked like it was made out of some sort of cheap man-made fibre, was covered in blood. As my mother did her best to clean her up, Dorothy fixed her with a reflective stare; she hadn't seen my mother for a number of years when they were both vibrant young women. They had both aged considerably. Shaking her head at the sad realisation she said, 'Look at us two old bastards.' As we drove to Swansea she took a £20 note from her purse. 'It's for the petrol,' she said. 'I don't want it,' I said. When I refused to take the money, I thought she would rip it up and chuck it out of the window, in true La Squires style, but she didn't. She insisted that she had money. Then, pulling out a double CD from her bag, told me she had just done a deal with a record company to re-release her Live London Palladium Concerts and could afford to pay her way. I insisted:

I don't want your money. How long have we been friends, Dot? You took me into your home, treated me like one of the family, you put me on the Palladium and made it possible for me to play every major theatre in the country. You gave me my first opportunity to record at Decca, which was instrumental in getting me a recording contract, and *now* you expect me to take money for petrol?

Dorothy put the money back in her purse and in an almost inaudible whisper said, 'I suppose so.' I took the CD from her and inserted it into my car CD player. As the soaring strings of Nicky's fabulous arrangements transported us back to those heady days at the Palladium, I reflected on how we were back then – full of ambition, when everything seemed to be possible. I glanced at Dorothy; she was smiling. It was sad to see her now, but for the moment at least, she was happy. As I watched this frail shadow of her former self, listening to the CD, I decided there and then to document the whole story before it was too late. I went to the BBC in Cardiff and convinced them that this was a story worth telling. They agreed and furnished me with a DAT tape recorder, which was used in those days, because of its broadcast quality. I had a hard time convincing Dot to talk to me about her life on tape; she was even more paranoid and suspicious of the media now than before. But, seeing that I had her best interest at heart, she agreed.

19

The Recording

When I arrived back at the house in Trebanog, I found her in the kitchen. The place was a mess – unwashed dishes in the sink, newspapers everywhere. Dot was frantically photocopying newspaper articles on the Rank Xerox photocopy machine in the middle of the room. She said she needed the copies for evidence – 'Don't Ask!' I started to set up the recording equipment on the kitchen table for the interview. 'Just a minute,' she said, 'I have to feed the cat.' When she opened the back door the sight that greeted us was a cornucopia of seething slimy slugs that had commandeered the cat's bowl and chomped their way through the remains of the Kitty Kat. This vision only added to the already seediness of Dot's surroundings and I was even more determined that the world should remember her for what she was and not what she had become. 'This will be your pension, John,' she said. 'No Dot,' I said, 'your legacy.' I hit the button and the interview commenced.

I soon realised that it wouldn't be an easy task. Dorothy always jumped from subject to subject; it was as if her mind was travelling faster than her mouth but now that she was in her 80s she was even more scatterbrained and confused than before, mixing the stories of yesteryear with those of last week.

I had to keep pulling her back to the point. When I listen to those tapes now I realise that I should have spoken less and just let her get on with it but I had no option; without me bringing her back to the story it would have been totally incomprehensible to anyone else.

We spoke for almost 5 hours in all. Most of the story I knew, either from first-hand experience or from stories my father had told me. A lot more unfolded as we talked well into the night and it struck me that perhaps now, years later, the truth can be told about her.

To this day the program hasn't been transmitted; the producers I contacted showed interest at first but when it went up to the fourth floor, it was always turned down. Dorothy always maintained that she was on a BBC blacklist. I didn't believe there was such a thing until a whistle blower, who hated what he was doing, told the *Observer* newspaper, who then printed a list of blacklisted people. One of those blacklisted is a friend of mine, Paul Turner, an editor who became a very talented director. He told me that every time he went for an interview for a promotion he was always turned down. It transpired that because he had been a member of the communist party and a supporter of 'Cymdeithas yr Iaith' (The Welsh Language Society) he was deemed to be a subversive. Nothing could have been further from the truth. He was a Cornishman who had learnt to speak Welsh to support a Welsh culture that was in danger of becoming lost to the world. But, justice prevailed and Paul went on to direct the Oscar-nominated Welsh film *Hedd Wyn*. And so you see, Dorothy wasn't as paranoid as people thought; when she said the BBC wouldn't play her records because she was on a blacklist, she was probably right. Who knows where fantasy ended and reality began with Dorothy. One thing is for sure, it was probably her own fault for getting embroiled in the Payola Scandal all those years ago, which to be fair would have been reason enough for the BBC to blacklist her.

Church Village Hospital

I don't remember if it was Esme or Peter who rang me to tell me that Dot was back in hospital; she'd fallen and broken her hip. This time there was no Roger to pick up the bill and she had to settle for the dear old NHS. She was in a pitiful state. She seemed much smaller somehow, frail. All her old feisty spark was gone; it was as if she'd given up. A jobsworth of a male nurse came in to the room and told her that she couldn't keep having visitors out of visiting hours. She fixed him with an icy stare and said: 'Do you know who this is? If it wasn't for his father I wouldn't have been in show business now fuck off.' A spark of the old Dot – she was still in there somewhere – but the writing was on the wall.

It wasn't long before Dot was in hospital again, this time it was in Llwynypia. She was, as usual, manically photocopying her press cuttings, when she was struck by a searing pain in her stomach. She managed to get to the phone and dial for help before collapsing.

When Esme and Dr Bali arrived they found Dorothy, face contorted with pain, lying semi-conscious on the floor. Dorothy explained that she couldn't pee. The doctor instructed Esme to get some towels from the bathroom, and set about alleviating the symptoms. She made her as comfortable as possible and insisted that she must go for her scan, explaining that she couldn't be responsible if she refused to get treated again – she'd missed four appointments already. The bleeding didn't sound good and the doctor stressed that time was of the essence. Dorothy, belligerent as usual, protested that there was nothing wrong. She eventually capitulated and went to see the specialist. It turned out that the cancer had returned. She, being in complete denial, totally rejected this diagnosis and started ranting that there was nothing wrong with her and that he, the specialist, had no right to tell her it was cancer; it was only haematuria. Dorothy had been self-diagnosing for years but this time was different; it was malignant and in her heart she knew it.

I decided to ring Emily, she was her next of kin after all, but I didn't know how to contact her; her old number had been discontinued. I asked Dot if she knew where she was. She told me that she was living in Brighton with her mother but she hadn't spoken with her for a while. She gave me Emily's new number and I called her. Em thanked me for ringing and told me that she knew of the situation because Peter had rung her and she promised she would come as soon as she could. Contrary to general opinion, Emily had always been there for Dorothy whenever she needed her and fully intended to come as soon as she could make arrangements for someone to look after her mother. Joyce had just had a knee replacement in the Royal Stanmore Hospital. She explained that it had been difficult, not least because she didn't know where Dorothy was. Now that she knew, she would come at once. Des and Peter came to the rescue once again, insisting that Emily stay with them at their house in Port Talbot.

On 28 March 1998, Emily arrived at my house with Peter. She told me she was terrified of a repeat performance of the last time she'd lived with Dorothy. She had moved in to support her, as the trauma of the Payola trial had exacerbated Dorothy's anxiety disorder; Emily had almost had a nervous breakdown herself. She was terrified of it happening again but realizing how ill Dorothy was she decided to travel to Wales to support her ailing aunty until her final sad demise.

Llywnypia Hospital

On a snowy March day in 1998, Emily made the trek over the bleak snow-covered Bwlch Mountain from Port Talbot to the Rhondda Valley. She made this arduous journey each day, not knowing if that day would be Dorothy's last. When she arrived at Llwynypia, she wasn't too pleased to find that Esme Coles had been put down as Dorothy's next of kin. Whether Dorothy did this to spite the family, whom she thought had deserted her, I don't know but Dorothy's actual next of kin at that time would have been her sister Rene. Emily told the receptionist, that whoever Esme Coles was she was defiantly *not* Dorothy's next of kin; her Aunty Rene was and as Rene was almost 90 years old by now and housebound, she was next in line.

When Emily entered the single private room, Dorothy's eyes lit up. Then, eyeing Emily up and down, she said, not too politely, 'You're too fat!' Emily smiled and retorted, 'Nice to see you too.' I went with Emily as often as I could but the meetings weren't easy; Dot was becoming more and more incoherent and muddled as her illness progressed. Her mind would wander back and forth, mixing and punctuating her sentences with the odd Welsh word. Most Welsh people can say a few words in the language, even if they don't speak it fluently but I was taken aback when I heard Dorothy speaking Welsh to the nurse. I thought that it was just some random sentence she'd remembered from her early days in Llanelli. Intrigued, I decided to test her and asked her, in Welsh, about her past life. Welsh can be a complicated language; there are myriad ways of saying yes and no for instance, so when Dorothy answered me with 'Naddo', the past tense of no, this proved to me, that as a young girl, Welsh must have been her mother tongue. I don't know why I should have been surprised by this revelation. Although Dorothy had lived in London for most of her adult life, it was obvious to me that she had never forgotten her Welsh roots. My grandfather, who was a Welsh-speaking Welshman, told me that when Dorothy lived with him and my grandmother in London, Dorothy would often ask him to tell her stories in Welsh because she was homesick. Emily told me that Dorothy came from a Welsh-speaking family. Dorothy's mother, her Auntie Lizzy, her Auntie Martha, Dorothy's elder sister Rene and her brother Freddie all spoke the language. Emily still remembers, with love, the Welsh folk songs that her father, Freddie, would sing to her whilst putting her to bed.

In one of Dorothy's more coherent moments I asked her why she hadn't called me for help when she was made bankrupt. She hit the roof saying she hadn't been made bankrupt, insisting that the house was still hers and she was going back there.

When I tried to explain to her that the house had been sold and turned into flats to pay off her debts, she broke down. Then, pointing an accusatory finger towards heaven, she whispered, 'What have I ever done to you?' Trying to comfort her, I said she'd feel better when she got out of hospital. There was a look of panic, no, fear in her eyes – she didn't want to go back to Esme's.

'I'm selling my jewellery. I can move,' she said, 'I don't want to sing anymore, John. I have no need for the gowns either but seeing them taken to Sotheby's with my jewellery was very emotional; I broke my heart, Johnny, but it was ridiculous to keep them. I was paying a fortune in insurance.'

In a state of desperation she had instructed Mike Terry to arrange for Sotheby's of London to auction off all her jewellery and expensive gowns. I can only imagine how hard it was to part with these, some of which were gifts from Roger and her devoted fans. Some of the beautiful items that went under the hammer were:

241 A diamond bracelet set with circular cut diamond: valued at £4,000.

242 A 14ct ruby and diamond bracelet of scroll and buckle shaped linking set with circular cut diamonds and rubies in three coloured 14ct gold: valued at £700

243 A cultured pearl and diamond necklace – the uniform cultured pearl necklace supporting a pendant designed as the initial d on a detachable circular cut diamond set clasp: valued at £800

244 A diamond pendant designed as a pear shaped line of circular cut diamonds supporting a single stone claw-set swing centre, on 18ct white gold chain: valued at £450

245 A diamond pendant designed as 'dot' set with circular-cut diamonds mounted within an abstract border of brick pattern linking, on a necklet chain reverse inscribed: 'the most wonderful night of our life, London Palladium 6th Dec 1970, love Jimmy and Len': valued at £800 [The pendant was given to Dorothy Squires by two of her ardent admirers after her triumphant concert at the London Palladium.]

246 A diamond ring designed as an abstract cluster, claw-set with circular-cut and marquise-shaped diamonds, the largest circular-cut stone set in the centre: valued at £2,500

247 An opal doublet and diamond ring designed as a twin cluster set with oval opal doublets and circular cut diamonds: valued at £1,500

248 A diamond ring set with circular-cut diamonds within an abstract mount of navette links: valued at £500

249 A gold, ruby and diamond wristwatch the rectangular dial concealed by a hinged calibré-cut ruby and eight-cut diamond set cover mounted between similarly set buckle shaped shoulders, mounted in 14ct gold length 163mm: valued at £1,200

250 A 9ct gold bracelet of fancy oval linking supporting a circular pendant depicting St Christopher: valued at £400

251 A ruby and diamond ring designed as an abstract cluster claw-set with cushion shaped diamonds and circular-cut rubies within textured wirework mount: valued at £3,000

252 A cultured pearl and ruby ring mounted with three cultured pearls within an abstract textured wirework mount decorated with circular-cut rubies: valued at £450

254 A fresh water pearl, ruby, emerald and lapis lazuli scarf consisting of ten rows of fresh water pearls terminating with lapis lazuli a' ruby and an emerald each bead alternating with south Indian fluted beads: valued at £4,000

255 A diamond ring, the brilliant-cut diamond weighing 3.80ct in a square mount accompanied by service public du controle des diamantes, perles fines, pierres precieuses. Paris number 131.671 stating j colour, vsi clarity case: valued at £11,000

256 A pearl, emerald and diamond necklace designed as four graduated rows of pearls on a cabochon emerald and diamond cluster clasp shortest strand, including clasp approximately 400mm long: valued at £12,000

257 A sapphire and diamond ring of heart shape design set with calibre cut sapphires within a border of' brilliant-cut diamonds: valued at £600

258 A gem-set cluster ring of stylised flower head design set with variously cut emeralds, sapphires, rubies and diamonds: valued at: £1,000

259 A sapphire and diamond ring of stylised ribbon bow set with an oval mixed-cut sapphire, calibre-cut sapphires and brilliant cut diamonds: valued at £800

260 A diamond pen annular bangle designed as a hinged cuff, decorated in a basket weave pattern and trimmed with brilliant-cut diamonds: valued at £3,500

Not everything from her collection was sold. What did sell, however, raised over £35,000. She had enough money to go anywhere now but somehow she had lost her confidence. It was catch-22; she didn't want to go back to Esme's but the thought of another move was even more daunting. Suddenly, remembering there was some of the jewellery in her handbag, she said: 'Get my bag, John, my building society book is in it. Ask the nurse.' On finding the nurse, she informed me that she'd given the bag to the lady who brought Dorothy in, for safe keeping because it had her wedding ring, her passport and some jewellery in it. When I told Dorothy she exploded: 'She had no right to give her my handbag.' She yelled, 'You'll have to get it back, John. Take Emily with you.'

When we arrived at the chip shop a hostile Esme confronted us. Her husband was hovering behind her. It was obvious by her manner she was not going to let us in. I told her that we'd only come for Dorothy's handbag and she had no right to withhold Dorothy's possessions from us; Emily *was* her next of kin after all. Esme told us that it was her house and that she could do what she liked. I exploded. 'Are you telling me that you are refusing to let her niece have her belongings? Is that what you're saying?' 'Huh! Some niece,' was her terse repost. 'Where were you when she needed you? I was the only one to give her a home.' 'Some home,' I retaliated, 'she told me you left her food on the doorstep like a dog.' 'She's lying,' she retaliated, 'she was a recluse; she wouldn't come out or open the door to anyone. I think she's nuts.' Realising we were getting nowhere with the intransigent Esme, I suggested we go but Emily was adamant; she was going nowhere until she'd retrieved Dorothy's belongings. 'Christ there's four mink coats in there for starters,' she said, 'then there are the master tapes and God knows what else. And where's her bloody handbag?'

Esme, unmoved by this broadside, ordered us out of her shop. I told her we'd get out of her shop but we would be back; what she was doing was illegal. Not sure of our legal rights, but determined, we left and headed for the police station. The local police station turned out to be a house manned by a single copper. I knocked at what looked like a small serving hatch and explained the situation to the local bobby. Raising his eyebrows, he informed us that he knew Esme of old and, in his opinion, we'd get nowhere with her. She'd been in a battle with her brothers for years over the house where Dorothy had been living. Allegedly, Esme's father had left the house between Esme and her brothers and she wouldn't let them in either. The policeman advised us to get a court order. Then, as a parting shot, he said, 'I think you're on dodgy ground though.'

When we got back to the hospital Emily contacted my solicitor, Barry Jones, and asked if he could arrange a court order. Barry contacted us later to say a court order wouldn't be necessary; he'd been in contact with Esme, who was still refusing entry, which was her right, but Dorothy's belongings would be outside ready to be collected. When Emily and Barry's clerk arrived at the house they were met by a brazen Esme. Outside the house there were fourteen suitcases and a number of black bags. Esme looked on in icy silence as Emily, with the solicitor's clerk, sifted through them. Emily found Dot's handbag and opened it – it was empty save for a building society passbook and some valium; there was no sign of her wedding ring. Shooting Esme a distrustful look, she opened a suitcase; it was stuffed with photocopies of Dorothy's court cases. She opened another and another; they were all stuffed with photocopies. Not satisfied, Emily demanded to know where the rest of her things were; there was no sign of the master tapes or her mink coats. Esme tersely informed her that that was all there was – Mike Terry had the master tapes and Dorothy wanted her to have the coats for looking after her. 'She didn't want any of the family to have them,' she said, 'they'd only pawn them. Anyway, she owed me a fortune in rent.' Emily, taken aback by this, said that she thought the house had been offered to Dorothy rent free. 'That was until I found out she had money; she wasn't as broke as she made out; she was getting a load of money in royalties.' It seems that Esme wasn't the Good Samaritan some people had made her out to be as this article in the *Daily Express* Hickey Column seems to imply:

NOW SQUIRES IS REALLY OUT ON HER OWN

As the last of the diamonds go under the hammer at Sotheby's this afternoon, Dorothy Squires is hoping to pocket enough cash to solve a tricky housing shortage. Squires the sometime spouse of Roger Moore, who's warbling ruled the post-war hit parade, has been ordered out of her latest refuge in Trebanog, South Wales.

She has been living in the £100,000 house rent free since June 1995 but now its owner, local fish and chip shop proprietress, Esme Coles has tired of Dot's reclusiveness. 'Esme can't get into her own house,' reports my boyo in the Rhondda Valley. 'Dorothy locks the door from the inside and won't open it to anyone. She spends most of the time in bed. Esme has told her to find somewhere else.'

Dorothy, 82 next Tuesday and once a millionairess, has already moved four times since being evicted from her Thames-side mansion in 1988. I would offer her a berth at Hickey Towers but fear her cats will upset Caesar.

When we arrived back at the hospital, Dorothy had taken a turn for the worse. A nurse, supporting her head, was holding a glass of water to her mouth. She swallowed the water, flopped back onto the pillow, then gazing up at the nurse through watery eyes whispered, 'Am I dying nurse?' The nurse looked at the frail figure in the bed and said, 'We're all dying Dot.' It would be a few more weeks before the inevitable happened and all we could do was wait. Emily asked the doctor how long Dorothy had: 'I know you are not God,' she said, 'but with your experience you must have a good idea.' With solemn face he told her that he didn't expect her to last the weekend. Although she was fading fast, there were still some lucid moments. With tears in her eyes, she said:

> I was worth two and a quarter million in cash and they put me out in the street, John. But, despite it all … all they have done to me, I still believe in God. I believe it was the man upstairs who brought me back to Wales. I pray to him and I say – I don't deserve the way I've been treated. I've helped so

many people; my family, my friends. All I've ever done was try to do good for everybody. I pray to God and I say – let me sort things out before I go. I didn't deserve to end like this; I was never cruel to anybody; I looked after my family and my old friends when I made it big. Many nights I cry myself to sleep; especially after talking to you last night, Johnny. It brought back so many memories. I have one ambition left; I want a sanctuary for retired racehorses. The reason I want to do it is because of poor Norwegian Flag.

Dorothy was drifting in and out of consciousness when an unexpected phone call was taken by the nurse – it was Roger Moore. The flustered nurse rushed into the room spluttering that Roger Moore was on the phone but she didn't know what to say. Taking the phone from her, Emily quipped, 'Hello would have been nice.' Roger asked after Emily's mother, Joyce, and spoke of his concern for Dorothy as his mother had suffered the same fate. Then in a kind and tender voice, he told Emily to take Dorothy's hand, squeeze it and tell her that Rog was thinking of her. He insisted that Emily contact him, should the inevitable happen. Unbeknown to any of us, Roger had been in touch with Dorothy during her final months. While being quizzed by Piers Morgan on TV, Roger recalled:

> Toward the end of Dorothy's life in 1989, we spoke on the telephone. We both agreed that we'd shared some great and happy times together. Dot said she was pleased that I had now found happiness with Christina, my fourth wife. She said, 'She's the one, Roger, isn't she?' 'Yes Dot,' I said, 'she really is.'

Emily, returned to the room, took Dorothy's hand and relayed Roger's message. Dorothy opened her eyes looked up at her in a mixture of disbelief and expectancy. The look that passed between them was a look of recognition that the love of her life still cared. Esme arrived soon after and Dorothy, feigning bravado, said, 'Hi Esme, that bastard Roger has just rung,' but the sardonic smile on her face betrayed her true feelings. After the break-up, Dorothy's life had been dominated by the pursuit of getting Roger back and that phone call was, to her at any rate, confirmation that he still had feelings for her and that what they had in the early days was true love and not, as the urban myth would have it, Roger using her influence in show business to further his career.

A couple of days after that phone call, Dorothy lost her fight for life, Emily lost her Auntie Dorothy, I lost one of my closest friends and the world of show business lost a great performer. Dorothy Squires died peacefully at Llwynypia Hospital on 14 April 1998.

Dorothy left this world still in the headlines, and still continues to appear in the tabloids to this day. If anyone thought that this would be the end to the Dorothy Squires saga, they were sadly mistaken. The litigation that had dogged her till the end was to rumble on and another legal battle was to ensue, this time over the royalties from Dorothy's entire musical catalogue. It was a considerable body of work; she'd written and recorded hundreds of songs, most of which she had bought back from the record companies, principally Decca International and President Records. Like all icons of showbiz when they die their records sales soar. This was true of Dorothy's records and record stores in Cardiff were inundated with fans trying to buy her albums.

Dorothy died intestate so her final wishes were never recorded and the vultures were circling. An acrimonious battle began over Dorothy's belongings between the family, Esme Coles and Mike Terry. It was Mike, who on returning from Spain, had written on a napkin instructions purporting to be Dorothy's last wishes, which allegedly gave him the royalties to all her musical recordings. He was also alleging that Esme was withholding property that was rightfully his. Little did Mike know that Emily had in her possession a will that Dorothy had made after Roger had left, leaving two thirds of her total possessions to Rene, her sister and one third to Emily. This was done in a fit of piqué to make sure her unfaithful husband didn't get a penny. The will was not produced; it was deemed invalid because one of the witnesses, Betty Newman, was also a beneficiary and a witness cannot inherit, although it would have proven Dot's intentions at the time.

Mike was adamant that Dorothy had given all her master tapes to him and he was convinced that because he had the aforementioned tapes in his possession, that he owned the copyright. Nothing could have been further from the truth. She had only given them to him for safe keeping after she left Leeds for South Wales. Mike accused Esme of hanging on to Dot's possessions, which he alleged she had promised him: a photocopier, Dorothy's master tapes and metal work of her recordings that had been re-edited ready for marketing. He was also demanding the master tapes, album and the printed copy of the stage play of the musical *Old Rowley* that had been penned by Dot, Ernie Dunstall and Mark Eden; none of these items were legally his save for the photocopier. (The copyright of *Old Rowley* is still the property of Ernie and Mark.) Last but not least, Mike was demanding she hand over a diamond pendant designed as 'DOT', set with circular-cut diamonds mounted on a gold chain that hadn't sold at auction which Mike had brought back to Dorothy. Esme swore she didn't have it. I don't know what happened to that pendant but one thing's for sure, it's not with its rightful owner, Emily Squires.

When Mike accused Esme of withholding his property she wrote to her solicitor to complain, a copy of which was sent to Mike. It transpires that, on returning from Spain, Mike had contacted Esme, demanding she return his property and made veiled threats that he had witnesses who would swear on oath that he had been bequeathed them by Dot. It is a well-known fact that Dot died intestate, leaving no such instructions. Mike was relying on a letter that Dorothy had sent him that read, 'to my dear friend, what would I have done without you! May you live long to enjoy all that I have bequeathed you.' He mistakenly took this as affirmation of Dorothy's intention to pass all her intellectual property to him.

Indeed, Dorothy may have promised that he could have them; she was notorious for making promises that she had no intention of fulfilling. I've no doubt she meant it at the time but by the next day all was forgotten and life went on as usual. But Mike took her promises literally and tried to pursue Emily through the courts. I don't know who advised him to take this misguided course of action but anyone who knows anything about copyright law will tell you that once a musical work has been lodged with the Performing Rights Society, unless that work had been signed over to another person in the writer's lifetime – and Dorothy did no such thing – it automatically goes to the next of kin and cannot be transferred. This letter from the Performing Rights Society also backs this up:

Our ref: KEF/wjs Your ref:
Ms Emily J. Squires
22 Wilbury Gardens

Karen Fishman
Corporate Counsel
Telephone: 020 7306 4541 Fax: 020 7306 4040 e-mail
karen.fishman@mcps-prs-alliance.co.uk

16 May 2003

Dear Ms Squires
Dorothy Squires deceased
Lost and Found, With All My Heart, White Wings, Blue Blile Blue, Clackers ("the Works")
Thank you for your letter of 29 April 2003 in connection with the above. As requested, I am writing to confirm my colleagues' advice that you would not be able to transfer to Mr Terry the performing right (or any part thereof) in the Works. On joining the Society your late aunt assigned her performing right interest in each of the Works to the Society and under the terms of our Articles of Association and your membership, ownership of those rights remains vested in the Society and cannot be assigned by you to any other person.

This didn't deter Mike from pursuing Emily through the courts, which resulted in her nearly having a nervous breakdown – she'd been through this type of ordeal innumerable times with Dorothy and now it was as if it was happening all over again. Mike sent letters to the Performing Rights Society,

MCPS, President Records, Sanctuary Records and EMI records, instructing them not to pay Emily any royalties. This was ludicrous as he was soon to find out. PRS and MCPS informed him that in no way was he entitled to any of Dorothy's royalties as they had never been officially signed over to him in her lifetime.

Some of the royalties he was claiming were not even written by Dot but by Billy Reid, who'd sold his royalties to someone else when he'd been at low ebb. Suffice it to say Mike's case against Emily was thrown out of court and Mike was told by the judge that if he wanted to pursue it further he would have to take it to the High Court, which would cost a considerable amount of money and the outcome was by no means certain. In his opinion it would be better for the two sides to come to some amicable agreement.

In my view, had Dorothy really wanted to gift the royalties of her entire catalogue to Mike, she would have signed it over during her lifetime. Emily tried in vain to get Mike to return the tapes; Dorothy's whole musical history was in them after all and she didn't want them lost or destroyed. But Mike was adamant, they were his and he even threatened to burn them before he would hand them over. Emily, naturally worried that he would carry out his threat, capitulated against better advice, I might add, and came to some kind of agreement with him.

She needn't have worried. It was well known that Eddie Kassner always made duplicate copies of all his recording sessions. In any event he would have had mint first pressings from which her albums could have been remastered. But because Mike produced a letter from Dorothy, purporting to give him the royalties to the so-called Polygon Tapes, Emily let him keep them and reap, during his lifetime, 90 per cent of the profits from the sales of any further pressings. She didn't have to do this as the letter from Castle Music confirms:

CASTLE LIMITED
A29 Barwell Business Park
Leatherhead Road
Chessington Surrey
KT9 2NYlei:
020 8974 1021 • Fax: 020 8974 2674/2880
intoocastlemusic.com website: www.castlernusiccom

Emily Jane Squires
Flat One
22 Wilbury Gardens
Hove
West Sussex
BN3 6HY

April 19, 2000
Dear Ms Squires

Thank you for your letter dated 3 April.

The so-called 'Polygon' recordings were owned by Pye Records and were originally released on the Polygon label, hence the name. The recordings owned by Pye were sold a few times and were eventually acquired by Castle in 1989. Your aunt did try to claim ownership of the Polygon titles but this was always disputed. Castle has accounted royalties to your aunt in respect of these recordings.

We saw the document under which Mr Terry claimed ownership. We were not prepared to accept his claim to ownership. We did confirm that your aunt could give someone the benefit of her royalties in the recordings but we asked for confirmation that the Estate was not disputing the document he had supplied. We only accept therefore that the Estate has directed us to pay royalties otherwise due to the Estate to Mr Terry on the 'Polygon' recordings. We still maintain that we own the copyright in the recordings and that your aunt had no right to try and transfer any kind of ownership to Mr Terry.

I hope this clarifies the position and if you have any queries please contact us. We are paying royalties to Mr Terry on the 'Polygon' recordings but these are minimal in any event. For example, the last half yearly payment was £72.

Yours sincerely
Judi O'Brien
Head of Legal Affairs

I have *some* sympathy for Mike; knowing how Dorothy could offer you the world one minute then totally forget it the next. But I have more sympathy for Emily who, while still mourning her Auntie Dorothy, had to go through a traumatic confrontation that she'd neither asked for nor needed.

20

The Funeral

Dorothy never did things by halves and in the true showbiz tradition she had two funerals: a Provincial opening and London for her final resting place. Emily decided that Dorothy should be buried in one of her beautiful cocktail dresses trimmed with ostrich feathers so that she could make her exit in true showbiz style. Unfortunately, all Dorothy's clothes were still at 'the house of tears', and Emily knew that she would have to confront Esme once again to get them. She went with Peter to the house in the hope that Esme would find it in her heart to let her in but she was denied entry once again. Dorothy's last home at Trebanog remained locked, while letters of administration were obtained to administer her estate. And so, Dorothy, who had always been known for her extravagant gowns, had to take her final curtain call in a simple undertaker's shift.

All the disputes seemed to melt away in the overwhelming 'Hiraeth' as Dorothy's recording of 'Song of the Valley' greeted the arrival of her rose-laden coffin. The first funeral service was held at St Mary's church, Port Talbot, on Tuesday 21 April and the interment at London's Streatham Park Cemetery three days later. Both attracted packed congregations. Dot's lifestyle song

'My Way' was played to loud applause and standing ovations at the close, in true London Palladium style. Lord Delfont once saluted her as the 'Iron Lung of Show Business' and the drawing power from her ever-loving fans was never disputed. This was underlined on a wet and windy Port Talbot, with nearly 500 people packed into St Mary's church with hundreds more waiting outside in the rain.

The choice of West Wales upset Mrs Esme Coles and she boycotted both funerals. She felt that, as she had provided Dorothy with a home in the Rhondda for the last three years, she should have been buried in Trebanog. Was that the real reason or did Esme still want to bask in Dorothy's reflected glory? As it happened she was conspicuous by her absence! My biggest regret was that I couldn't be at either ceremony; I was performing on a cruise ship in the Caribbean at the time. So, my actress wife Olwen Rees recited 'All is Well' on my behalf; actor and friend Sion Probert boomed out Dylan Thomas's 'And Death Shall Have No Dominion' and Stan Stennett, who also appeared on that magical night at the Palladium, gave a moving speech. 'Dorothy never did things by halves,' he said. 'This is in true show business tradition – opening in the provinces then on to London.' After the tributes, the Reverend Stephen Barnes called for a standing ovation as the coffin was wheeled out to start the journey to London.

The London funeral that Emily had arranged for Dorothy was one that she would have been proud of – 200 of Dorothy's family and friends and devoted fans travelled to Streatham Park cemetery to say goodbye to the Welsh diva. One person conspicuous by his absence was Roger Moore; although another James Bond, George Lazenby, who had nothing to do with Dorothy, bizarrely turned up. Mark Eden turned up, but at the wrong cemetery. The capacity crowd that greeted the coffin as it entered St George's chapel heralded a fitting finale for the showbiz legend. Emily Squires had arranged to get a small digital piano into the chapel, and Russ Conway, who had played on Dorothy's self-written hit 'Say It With Flowers', had the full house singing along with it and later paid his own personal tribute to Dorothy:

With all that's been said about Dorothy Squires, let us not forget her sense of humour. It was tremendous and many of us who were very close to her personally and in the business can bear witness to some of the hilarious moments we shared in the theatres, backstage and sometimes even on stage, and also in the recording studios, where I have seen an entire orchestra almost drop their instruments on hearing one of Dorothy's off the cuff remarks, and roar with laughter. Only those of us close to her knew of her great kindness and thoughtfulness for others. When, sometimes, she had mountainous problems of her own, she was always ready to help others sort out their problems. Though she had no children, she possessed a motherly instinct, which manifested itself at such times. For me, I will remember some of the golden moments we worked together.

The evening at The Met, Edgware Road, when I was doing my very first week in variety at Dorothy's instigation, she was topping the bill and the friends gathered around falling apart with laughter as Dot showed and taught me how to apply stage make-up. A television sketch if ever there was one. Then again while in summer season in the Winter Gardens, Bournemouth, in 1965, when she and her retinue lodged themselves in the house I had rented there. No payment was required, but she left me with a huge pot of one of her own homemade stews. It lasted me the whole week.

As Dorothy's coffin was carried from St George's chapel by four fans, to be buried in the same grave as her only brother, Fred, she got another standing ovation. Fellow pros and fans from all over Britain truly said it with flowers; Streatham cemetery looked like the Chelsea Flower Show! Even ex-husband Roger Moore sent a wreath of purple tulips with a card that read 'I've said it with flowers, Roger' and Danny La Rue, Dot's great friend, wrote with his tribute, 'Shine brightly as ever, Dot'. Dress designer Douggie Darnell, representing Shirley Bassey, brought a huge oasis of white orchids, white lilies and carnations, ice-pink rosebuds and specially made white pearled ostrich feathers, Dot's trademark. It was truly a great send off as Dorothy took her final curtain call.

Emily wrote her farewell speech in the middle of the night, when she could no longer bear the images still being portrayed in the press about her Auntie Dorothy. She was more than just a singer who ended up as a penniless recluse *or* Roger Moore's ex-wife. She touched many lives with her talent and kindness, including myself. But most of all Dorothy loved Emily as the daughter she never had and it was her speech that left everyone with tears in their eyes, therefore I think it only fitting that I leave the last words to her:

Emily's Tribute

Over the past weeks I have heard my aunt talked about as the singer, the vexatious litigant, the penniless recluse. Recluse, yes, penniless, no. And the one the press seem to love most of all, Dorothy Squires the ex-wife of Roger Moore. But what about Dorothy the generous lady who opened her heart and her homes to so many people from all walks of life. She gave people a home when they had problems. That is why I will always be grateful to Esme Coles, her devoted fan, who gave her a home when the family couldn't. I want to tell you that Dorothy was an aunt too.

Aunty Dorothy, the larger than life lady, who on one occasion, to my embarrassment, picked me up from school wearing a mink coat and driving a large powder blue Thunderbird, the Aunty who sat in the front row of my school concert and cheered at my portrayal of Humpty Dumpty, and offered stage directions from the audience. The Aunty who knew I was unhappy as a boarder in my convent that I went to after my father died, so she rescued me on Sundays in the summer to splash around in her swimming pool along with twenty other 6–8 year olds and two nuns. Yes, nuns at Bexley, on these occasions she was a model of decorum, the nuns left without adding to their vocabulary. The Aunty who would lay awake at night, cuddle me and tell me of her life in Hollywood with numerous anecdotes. The Aunty who told me most men were not good, then constantly tried to match me with every available man, young and old. She was still trying to do this when she was ill in hospital. She used to remind me that at the age of three I stood on a chair, drew myself up to my full height, leaned over her large dining table and announced: 'Aunty Dorothy I love you.'

She then mimicked my stance and said and I love you Emily Jane. Words passed between us many times in the last few weeks. I know my Aunt did not always like me, she did not always approve of things I did, but I do know she loved me. Despite the rows and fights we had, we always made up. Despite the number of times I walked out, or was thrown out of Bexley and Bray, despite not seeing her for seven years, but still talking to her on the telephone wherever she was living, when I first saw her a month ago in hospital her eyes lit up and her arms opened wide for a hug, and she said, my Emily my lovely Emily. That's what I'll remember. Aunty Dorothy I know you are safe now, and may I say, thanks for the good times and the bad; I learnt from them. Thanks for the fun we had together. And thank you for so many fascinating memories; life with you was never dull. xxx

21

Epilogue

At the height of her career it was rumoured that Dorothy Squires was worth £2 million but because of her predilection for suing people, her fortune quickly depleted and along with it her credibility. In 1987 the Attorney General, Sir Michael Havers, made her a vexatious litigant. But contrary to public opinion Dorothy didn't die a bankrupt. She died intestate and in 1998 her remaining family inherited £30,000 and the royalties from her many recordings.

Index

You may also be interested in …

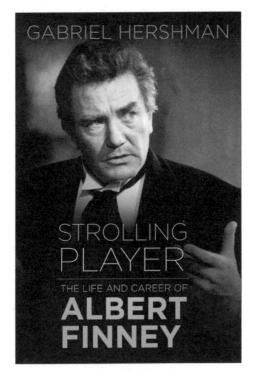

9780 7509 7886 6

Drawing on interviews with many of his
directors and co-stars, *Strolling Player*
examines how one of Britain's greatest
actors built a glittering career without
sacrificing his integrity.

The History Press

The destination for history
www.thehistorypress.co.uk

You may also be interested in …

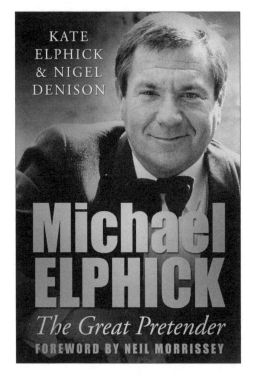

KATE
ELPHICK
& NIGEL
DENISON

Michael
ELPHICK
The Great Pretender
FOREWORD BY NEIL MORRISSEY

9780 7524 9147 9

'The book is remarkable for its candour.'
– *The Daily Mail*

You may also be interested in …

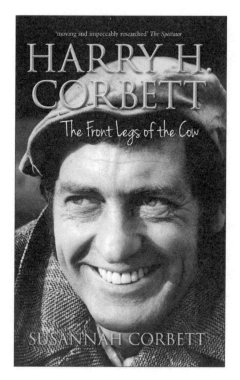

9780 7524 8787 8

Written by his daughter, Susannah, this
is the first biography of Harry H. Corbett,
the man who was once called 'the
English Marlon Brando'.

You may also be interested in …

9780 7509 6605 4

Bestselling author Michelle Morgan
accesses previously unseen documents
to tell the story of a woman whose
remarkable life and controversial death
continues to enthral.

The destination for history
www.thehistorypress.co.uk